Olivier, Olivier

SCRIPT AND DIRECTOR
Series Editor Inga Karetnikova

OLIVIER, OLIVIER

by Agnieszka Holland
(in collaboration with Régis Debray and Yves Lapointe)

Translated from the French by Gaile Sarma

HEINEMANN
Portsmouth, NH

Heinemann
A division of Reed Elsevier Inc.
361 Hanover Street
Portsmouth, NH 03801-3912
Offices and agents throughout the world

Library of Congress Cataloging–in–Publication Data

Holland, Agnieszka, 1948–
[Olivier, Olivier. English]
Olivier, Olivier / by Agnieszka Holland (in collaboration with Régis Debray and Yves Lapointe) ; translated from the French by Gaile Sarma.
p. cm.
ISBN 0–435–07003–7
I. Olivier, Olivier (Motion picture) II. Debray, Régis. III. Lapointe, Yves. IV. Title.
PN1997.041413 1996
791.43'72—dc20 96–26989
CIP

Printed in the United States of America on acid-free paper
98 97 96 DA 1 2 3 4 5 6

Contents

Foreword

Agnieszka Holland was born in Warsaw in 1948, shortly after Stalin had replaced Hitler as the master of Poland. Both of her parents were journalists. They named their daughter Agnieszka after the young heroine of a celebrated Polish epic novel, *Nights and Days*, who was defiant and independent. The name turned out to be prophetic.

Agnieszka was a sickly child, so she spent a lot of time in bed—a convenient place to draw and write, which she did obsessively. Somehow, most of what she was writing were short plays, which she would then "stage" with her little friends, herself always directing: "I liked to have the power of having people do things I wanted them to do," she recalls.

When she was thirteen, her father was arrested and accused of being a spy. It was one of those wild, false accusations typical of the KGB. Soon after his arrest, the family was informed that he had thrown himself out of a window during an interrogation, but relatives and friends had no doubt that he was murdered. This was a horrible shock for Agnieszka. "She wouldn't speak for weeks after that," her mother said.

With the name Holland—both notorious and Jewish (her father was Jewish, her mother is a Catholic)—Agnieszka's chances of being accepted into a cinema school in Poland were nil. So when she was seventeen, she sent her drawings and plays to the famous Czech Film Academy, and became one of seven applicants (out of two hundred and twenty) who were accepted.

In Prague she made her first film, the 25-minute *The Sin of God*, based loosely on a short story by Isaak Babel. It is a film about a prostitute who is constantly abused and impregnated by men. Desperate, she begs God to give her a man who is gentle and loving. God submits to her plea and sends her an angel. Promptly, she takes the angel into her bed, where, attempting to make love to him, she smothers and suffocates him to death. The anxiety and bleak humor of this early film would soon develop into the unmistakable "Holland touch."

In 1968, the year of the Prague Spring, Agnieszka was still at school, studying and making her short films. In Prague she met her future husband, a fellow student. "My philosophy at that time was that politics was less important than artistic life," she remembers, "but after one day in the student demonstrations I realized this was not true. Prague Spring was . . . like an artistic happening in its joyousness." There was the intoxication of a sudden freedom, and a hope that maybe, just maybe, Communism and liberty could, after all, be compatible.

They could not. The Soviet tanks rolled in and proved it. Holland, who had become very active in the student movement, was sentenced to a prison term. After several weeks in solitary confinement, she was released.

In 1971 she went back to Warsaw. Her activities in Prague had worsened her relations with the Polish authorities. She left Poland as a young girl, persecuted because of her father; she came back a young woman, an artist, and a persona non grata of her own standing. In a peculiar way, this gave her some grim satisfaction. "I wanted to have problems of my own choice," she says. She would have plenty.

In the following few years she wrote more than a dozen scripts. All were rejected by the authorities. This was an extremely trying time for her, as it was for many creative artists. Yet it was an exhilarating time also.

The 1970s—the so-called decade of stagnation in Eastern Europe and the Soviet Union—were, paradoxically, a decade of tremendous artistic creativity in these countries. Granted, the Communist regimes there were still highly oppressive and coercive, but no longer to the point of murder (that is, physically eliminating rebellious artists as had been done under Stalin). This allowed the artists—those who refused to be bought or coopted—an option to starve, but be independent. Which, in fact, was an option of poking holes in, making fun of, and, in general, undermining the regime by using Aesopian language and hints that everyone understood. The artists knew that what they were doing was crucially important for thousands, if not millions, of their countrymen, and it gave them the incomparable thrill of a life and death bond with their audiences.

Agnieszka was not allowed to make films in Poland, but her scripts were known, and her reputation was growing. In the late 1970s the political climate in Poland became very volatile. The democracy movement was rapidly gaining strength, making it possible for Andrzej Wajda, the grand master of the Polish cinema, to bring Agnieszka onto his creative team.

She started to do script-doctoring for him and was Wajda's First Assistant Director on his classic *Man of Marble*. He began to fight on her behalf. Wajda's efforts paid off. Finally, Agnieszka was permitted to make *Sunday Children* and *Film Tests*, two short (40 and 60 minutes) films, followed by two full-length features, *Provincial Actors* (1979) and *Fever* (1980), both considered rather important for the Polish cinema.

The film she made after that was called *A Woman Alone*—the tale of a single woman postal clerk who leads a wretched life, raising her young son in a dilapidated shack on the outskirts of town. The woman is dirt-poor, desperate, and angry. In fact, everyone in the film is desperate and angry: her son's father, a drunk and a bully; her current lover, a pathetic cripple; her neighbors, who make fun of the cripple. Even her young son: in one scene of the film, while she, exhausted, slumbers on her bed, the boy traps an insect crawling on the kitchen table and drops it into his mother's open mouth. She awakens, choking, enraged, grabs the boy and beats him senseless.

As someone noted, Holland pushed her microphones and her camera lenses right up to her characters' faces, making their voices harsh and their expressions grotesque, like some demented characters out of Brueghel. If this was her metaphor for life in Poland under the Communists, one wonders how she was able to shoot the film there. "It was shot during the high days of Solidarity, when even the censors went on strike," she chuckles.

Agnieszka was in Sweden promoting *A Woman Alone*, when, on December 12, 1981, in an attempt to crush the Solidarity movement, martial law was declared in Poland. Many of her filmmaker friends were beaten and thrown in jail. She was warned not to come back. Her film, *A Woman Alone*, was banned; soon it became an underground classic.

She went to Paris. She was thirty-three years old. Her "second" life had begun. Initially, though, it was not much different from the first; in some respects even worse. "I lost my family and friends' support, I didn't have any money, and I didn't speak the language," she recalls. And the most awful thing was that she was completely cut off and had no information about her husband and her nine-year-old daughter, who had remained in Warsaw. Unable to communicate with them, she kept vigils at the Paris airport, hoping against hope that they would be permitted to join her. After eight agonizing months, her daughter was allowed to leave Poland. Her husband was not. (Years later, when he could leave, he decided to remain in Poland.)

Determined to change her situation, Agnieszka plunged into work. Her energy was inexhaustible. She learned the language, began translating novels, then writing for French TV. In a few short years, Agnieszka Holland was able to succeed where many of her fellow expatriate directors failed—she came back to filmmaking.

In 1985 she completed *Angry Harvest*, her first film made in the West. Perhaps no two people could be further apart than the film's two characters: an uncouth, middle-aged, Polish Catholic farmer and a young, upper-class Austrian Jewish woman. Everything about them—their upbringing, way of life, habits, customs, education—are truly a world apart, and yet these two people are thrown together by vicious and deadly circumstances.

In a forest, the rough and moody farmer comes across a beautiful young woman who has just miraculously escaped from a train taking her and her family to Auschwitz. He brings her to his farm and, risking his life, hides her there from the Nazis. He is puzzled by her. To him she is like an exotic bird. He is much attracted to her, however, anti-Semitism is not entirely alien to him. So he is both fascinated and repulsed by her.

She, too, is fascinated by him—as the saved by the savior, and the captive (which, in a way, she is) by the captor. But she is also attracted to him as a man, attracted and repulsed.

In terms of external events, not much happens in the film. The gut-wrenching drama comes from the unpredictable shifts of the entangled passion and contempt the two people, trapped in a horrible world, feel toward each other. "Agnieszka has this great ability of getting "inside people," notes her French producer, Christian Ferry.

Angry Harvest was nominated for the Academy Award as the best foreign film, but it was not successful at the box office. Holland would have probably remained a director known only to movie buffs, were it not for a film she made a few years later, in 1991, called *Europa, Europa*.

Based on the remarkable true story of a German Jewish youth, Solly Perel (who looked more Aryan than many Aryans), the film follows Solly's trials from his initial escape during the "Kristall Nacht," through his journey into Poland, then into Russia, where he is made a member of the Young Communist League. Then, because of some incredible turns of events, he goes back into Germany where he ends up enrolled into an elite Nazi school, and finally, back again into Russia. The film ends with the real Solly Perel, now an old man, reciting a prayer in Israel.

When the film was released, it became a sensation. A highly controversial sensation, though. While in Europe it was accused of being false, inept, [and] anti-Semitic (Holland, who usually does not respond to her critics, wrote to the reviewer that she has suffered enough *from* anti-Semitism to now suffer the accusation *of* it). In the United States the film was extolled. Critics raved about it: it was named the best foreign film by the National Board of Review, and only the fact that Germany, where the film was made, didn't formally submit it for the

Academy Award prevented it from winning an Oscar. In the United States it also became an extraordinary box office success.

But *Europa, Europa* is not just a picaresque account of a youth trying to survive in an insane world. There is a scene in the film when, in his dream, Solly, who has experienced both Nazism and Communism, sees Hitler and Stalin waltzing tenderly together. There is absolutely no difference between Hitler and Stalin, between Nazism and Communism, Holland says, echoing George Orwell (except Orwell went even further, saying that those who claim that there *is* a difference are usually those who side with either one or the other).

And she makes another point: by calling her film *Europa, Europa*, she wants to emphasize that there are two Europes—one refined and civilized, the other prejudicial and murderous—intertwined forever.

Olivier, Olivier was her next film. Made in France in 1992, it was not, as she put it, "about Poles, Jews, nor politics." But it was also based on a true story. In a newspaper, Agnieszka had come across a report about the mysterious disappearance of a nine-year-old boy in a small French town, and his supposed return as a teenager six years later.

On the surface, *Olivier, Olivier* is less ambitious than *Europa, Europa*; after all, it is not about nations' tragedies, but a family's tragedy. As a film, though, it is more sophisticated: it delves deeper into human psychology; it is more compact than *Europa, Europa*, and thus structurally more unified.

However, when *Olivier, Olivier* was released, the critics' opinions were once again polarized. Some called the film "perverse," "subversive," "shocking and disorienting," and "the transmutation of incest into an acceptable love." Others praised it for its emotional generosity, sensuality, and intellect; they hailed the film as "profoundly religious," praised the director for her psychological storytelling, and even compared her to Dostoevsky.

Olivier, Olivier was a very personal film for Holland. She knows what a mother feels when separated forcibly from her child. When, after the military coup d'etat in Poland, she found herself alone in Paris with all means of communicating with her family cut off, she thought that she would never see her daughter again. She knew that, as someone noted, "for her daughter, she had disappeared, vanished, as abruptly as had Holland's own father." "When my daughter finally arrived in France, she could not speak to me," Holland recalls," adding "later, she told me she had been sure that I was dead."

Europa, Europa, Olivier, Olivier: the double titles are not an accident. Holland's own story can be called *Agnieszka, Agnieszka*. "Only I don't know if the double title would be enough," she says. "I was depressed after *Olivier, Olivier*," she continues. "The film was very tiring for me, even more than *Europa, Europa*."

Meanwhile, Hollywood studios were sending her piles of scripts about World War II and Berlin in the 1930s. But she didn't want to continue, as she put it, "painting black on black . . . I wanted to do something light and full of hope, after all the films I've done."

So, she was quite happy when she received an offer from Warner Brothers and Coppola's American Zoetrope to make a film based on Frances Hodgson Burnett's children's classic *The Secret Garden*. "When I was a child, *The Secret Garden* was one of my favorites," Holland says.

She read it then over and over again—this story of a determined ten-year-old girl, Mary Lennox, her wealthy, miserable uncle, her sickly cousin, and of the garden—once magnificent, but now locked up and neglected. Mary, by her sheer will and perseverance, rejuvenates the garden, revives her cousin, and turns her uncle's life around.

The Secret Garden is Holland's most optimistic film. Mary, the little girl, triumphs against nearly impossible odds .

Agnieszka Holland has made it. "I feel that I have the power to stay independent," she says. "I can do a movie for one million dollars, or I can do it for ten thousand." She now has several projects going on simultaneously in both Europe and America, and she is much in demand in Hollywood.

Is there any danger that she might get sucked in, commercialized by the system? Very unlikely. One who would not be subdued by the Communist apparatchiks, nor seduced by the European film bureaucracy, won't be corrupted by Hollywood glamour.

Now a personal note: Before meeting Agnieszka for the first time in New York, I knew that she had gone through a lot in her life, and that she had never accepted defeat. Thus, I expected to see a woman who would be, if not harsh, then very strong-willed and over-driven. She turned out to be nothing like that. She is calm, relaxed, not in the least a "professional" woman, but not a bohemian either. Just friendly, pleasant, and wise.

Leon Steinmetz

OLIVIER, OLIVIER

EXT. FRENCH COUNTRYSIDE IN THE 1980s. FOREST. DAY.

A foggy and rainy day in late summer. Two children—the boy 8 or 9 years old, the girl a little older—are playing in the grass and bushes of an old trench that dates from the First World War. OLIVIER and NADINE DUVAL—brother and sister—look very much alike: the same blond hair, the same light brown eyes, dressed in hooded capes of the same yellow. She seems more somber and serious than her brother, who looks confident and mischievous.

NADINE is crawling on her stomach, ahead of OLIVIER. She is obviously the leader. The boy, who is clumsier, drags himself behind her as best he can. She turns toward him.

NADINE: Go, move! We're going to run out of oxygen . . . . They have a chemical weapon, you know?
OLIVIER: Wait! I've got something in my shoe.

Irritated, NADINE sighs. She crawls toward OLIVIER and helps him take off one of his boots, which she shakes, dumping out a June bug. They observe the half-crushed insect, which tries to regain its footing.

OLIVIER: Is it an earthling?
NADINE: Don't be fooled, he's their transmitter. Do you see his antennas? We have to wipe him out!

She seizes a stone and crushes the June bug. Chagrin flits across the boy's face. He is on the verge of tears. NADINE hands him the shoe. OLIVIER puts it on, looking again at the insect in its death throes. NADINE resumes crawling forward.

NADINE: Hurry up, kid!

He throws himself on his stomach. Suddenly, she freezes, her gaze on a nearby clearing. She makes a sign to her brother to freeze in place, breath suspended. A noise coming from the path through the woods becomes more distinct: the crunch of bicycle wheels in the sand.

OLIVIER: What is it?
NADINE: A scout from the little green men. Look out, get ready. We can't get him angry. He has the death ray, too.

She takes a piece of plastic tube from the pocket of her rain-cape; OLIVIER immediately does the same. She puts the tube up to her left eye and looks through the opening at a young man in blue pedaling his bicycle. It is the Duvals' neighbor, MARCEL. With extreme concentration, NADINE narrows her eyes and aims. She imitates the noise of an explosion. OLIVIER looks back and forth from MARCEL to NADINE. As if struck by her gaze, MARCEL loses his balance and falls in a mud puddle. She turns triumphantly toward her brother.

NADINE: You saw it? I hit a bull's eye!

OLIVIER regards his sister with admiration and claps his hands. MARCEL gets up swearing, covered with mud, and the boy bursts out laughing. NADINE puts her hand over her brother's mouth to silence him.

NADINE: Shush!

They can't stop themselves from laughing quietly as they huddle together.

MARCEL gets up and rides away. OLIVIER pees in the man's direction.

OLIVIER (*singing*): "Pee-pee on the grass, to bug the ladybugs. Pee-pee on the grass, to bug the butterflies."

EXT./INT. GRANDMOTHER'S HOUSE. LIVING ROOM. MORNING.

SERGE—the father of the children—is getting down from his Renault 5 in front of his mother's house. He is a man of medium size, beginning to get a bald spot, with an expressive and nervous face. He enters the house. The living room is filled with old and shabby things. The OLD LADY, encumbered with very thick glasses and an over-sized set of false teeth, is struggling to move a sofa with a loose leg. SERGE knocks at the door, and enters without waiting for a response. At that moment the sofa falls on its back, nearly pulling his mother to the ground.

SERGE: Nothing broken, Mother?
OLD LADY: Yes, the foot.
SERGE: Show me.

She points to the foot of the sofa. The television set is on. In front of it is an enlarging screen, which makes the images blurry and confused.

SERGE kisses the OLD LADY and leads her away from the sofa. She is breathing heavily, her head is still shaking from her recent efforts. SERGE wants to take her pulse, but she briskly withdraws her hand.

OLD LADY: I'm not the one who's sick!
SERGE: Fine, so what's next?
OLD LADY: I just wanted to put the sofa near the window. That way, she'll be warmer. . . . If only you would take care of her. . . . I don't ask anything more.

SERGE sighs, and bends under the table to remove MIMI, an old and very fat female dog with short legs. He puts her under his arm, the animal's body dangling pitifully; with the other hand, he pushes the sofa against the window. He places the dog on the sofa and examines her professionally. The OLD LADY watches him.

SERGE straightens up and looks at his mother.

SERGE: This doesn't make any sense, Mother, you know it very well. You're only tormenting the dog. If you won't let me put her to sleep, at least leave her in peace.
OLD LADY (*in a sudden fit of anger*): Why don't you just say that you'd rather put us both to sleep! Lord Jesus Christ! And I thought your profession was healing, not killing!

SERGE: Okay, I'll give her an injection . . . but only if you let me take your blood pressure.
OLD LADY: I call that blackmail!
SERGE: If you like, it's blackmail.

The OLD LADY heaves a sigh of resignation. SERGE takes an ampoule and syringe from his case and leans over the totally passive animal. He sticks the needle in its foreleg.

The television is showing Mitterand's speech at a meeting.

OLD LADY: Look, these rotten fellows, the Social Communists, you like that, of course. . . . How long do we have to put up with them, these low-lifes. . . .

MIMI, revived by the injection, stands up on the sofa and barks hoarsely at the screen. The OLD LADY is delighted.

OLD LADY: You see? You see?

For an instant, the wavering image of Mitterand fills the enlarging screen. SERGE manages to take his mother's blood pressure.

SERGE: Mama, you absolutely must stay in bed for a few days, all right? I'll come by tomorrow evening and give you an injection . . .

She wants to protest, but SERGE doesn't allow her to talk.

SERGE: Doctor's orders. . . . Elizabeth or Nadine will bring you your meals. If it gets worse, phone me, all right?
OLD LADY: I don't like Elizabeth's cooking.
SERGE: I'll tell her to make her best stuff.
OLD LADY: And for Mimi, eggs . . . with liver, chopped fine.

From the doorway, SERGE shakes his head, resigned.

SERGE: No mistake, Mama. It's a promise. Chopped fine.

INT. DUVALS' HOUSE. OLIVIER'S/NADINE'S BEDROOMS. NIGHT.

OLIVIER is already in bed; his mother, ELIZABETH, is seated on the edge of his bed: she is talking to him, with a book on her lap. He has rewound his watch, which he places carefully on the bedside table. Through the huge, wide-open door between the two rooms, we see NADINE, who is about to go to bed. She stops by the door, and watches the two jealously.

OLIVIER: . . . And when you were little, did you like to go to school?
ELIZABETH: No, I always managed to catch a cold.
OLIVIER: How?
ELIZABETH: By walking barefoot in the snow, or going out with wet hair . . .
OLIVIER (*laughing*): But it's not nice to do that!
NADINE: Me, I love to go to school.
ELIZABETH: It's not the same for you, you're a model girl. I was only good at gymnastics.
NADINE: Olivier is no good in gym . . . he's the worst in his class.
ELIZABETH: He's still little . . .

She caresses the child's head with a special gesture, which messes up his hair.

OLIVIER: Mommy, do you believe in extraterrestrials?
ELIZABETH (*to Nadine*): Did you brush your teeth?

NADINE shows her teeth, which have braces on them. ELIZABETH looks at her for an instant and suddenly freezes, as if lost in her thoughts. NADINE, with her teeth still exposed, casts a glance at her brother. OLIVIER smiles at her in a superior way, and pulls at his mother's sleeve.

OLIVIER: Ma!

She doesn't react. The boy sits up in bed and passes his hand in front of his mother's eyes while blowing in her ear.

OLIVIER: Wake up, Mama . . . I'm here.

She returns to consciousness, blinks her eyes, and turns toward him with a smile that is still distracted.

ELIZABETH: Yes, my little dear . . .

OLIVIER: Are you back on earth?
ELIZABETH: Yes, as you say . . . I'm with you now. . . . Shall I read you a story?
NADINE (*from the other room*): No, sing instead. I can hear it better.
ELIZABETH (*to Olivier*): Which song would you like? "The Angels"?

OLIVIER nods. ELIZABETH turns out all the lights, except for a little bedside light.

ELIZABETH (*singing*): "The angels are stooping above your bed. . . . God's laughing in heaven to see you so good. . . . "

ELIZABETH caresses her son to the song's rhythm. OLIVIER closes his eyes blissfully. NADINE is lying, stretched out. Her eyes shine in the darkness. ELIZABETH sings more softly.

ELIZABETH: "I kiss you, I kiss you/For I must admit/I'll certainly miss you/When you're all grown up."

She kisses the boy.

ELIZABETH: Now go to sleep, my little lamb.

ELIZABETH gets up and goes to NADINE. She bends over her daughter and the girl hangs onto her tightly.

ELIZABETH: Good night, my big girl.

She frees herself from NADINE's grip and leaves the room. NADINE sits up in bed.

NADINE (*quietly*): Olivier! (*Silence.*) Are you sleeping, Olivier?
OLIVIER: No . . .
NADINE: Do you see them?
OLIVIER: No.
NADINE: Then turn off your lamp! You'll see some little lights . . . that turn on and off . . . on and off . . .
OLIVIER: I'm afraid . . .
NADINE: Idiot. . . . If you're afraid, they'll burn your eyes. They're worse than dogs. Dogs only bite when you're afraid, get it?

OLIVIER: Stop it.

His voice begins to tremble.

NADINE: They're gliding all around your bed. . . . Watch out! They're flying towards the door . . . Are they coming near you?

OLIVIER shuts his eyes as tightly as he can and presses his pillow against his head. NADINE laughs.

NADINE: Dummy! If you're afraid, you'll never see anything.
OLIVIER (*sobbing*): I'm going to tell Mommy that you make me afraid all the time . . .
NADINE: If you tell on me it's over, I'll never play with you again.

INT. DUVALS' HOUSE. PARENTS' ROOM. NIGHT.

Only the bedside lamps are on. SERGE and ELIZABETH, on either side of the double bed, are getting undressed mechanically, without looking at one another.

SERGE: Mama isn't at all well, you know. I had to insist that she take it easy for at least a few days . . .
ELIZABETH: You shouldn't leave her there alone anymore.
SERGE: You have a solution? She's so stubborn. . . . You've told me often enough that you can't stand her, right.
ELIZABETH: Yes, but . . .

She stops suddenly and freezes, looking at him absently as if in a trance, her stocking half off. He regards her with disapproval.

SERGE: What's the matter now?

Her eyes blink; she smiles, confused.

ELIZABETH: Nothing . . . I thought I heard Olivier crying.
SERGE: We'll have to have you examined. You're getting bizarre, you know . . . Sometimes you scare me. . . . I knew an epileptic once who. . . . It starts with these absences and then. . . . You shouldn't drive the car.
ELIZABETH: That's a lot of crap.

SERGE: Tomorrow we'll have to bring Mama her meal. Make her some eggs with some finely chopped liver, she adores it. You know her whims . . .
ELIZABETH: They're coming for the insurance tomorrow.
SERGE: You can send Nadine, or the little guy. It won't do them any harm. Anyway, kids don't do anything anymore in this country. More vacations than school.
ELIZABETH: . . . I thought I heard your mother . . .
SERGE: Not again with this nonsense . . .

ELIZABETH slides under the covers and opens a book. SERGE takes off his pants, from which a few coins fall and roll under the bed. He gets down on all fours and, passing his hand under the bed, he pulls out some curls of dust. He sneezes, retrieves the coins, and gets up.

SERGE: Look at this filth! Obviously no one sweeps under the bed.
ELIZABETH: What?
SERGE: Really, you're going too far. As if you had anything else to do but take care of the kids and the house!

ELIZABETH doesn't reply; she closes her book and puts out the light. In bed, she turns her back to SERGE.

ELIZABETH: Good night.

He turns out his bedside light also.

SERGE: Good night!

They lie for a moment in silence. Suddenly the door opens wide enough to admit OLIVIER, half–asleep, carrying his pillow. ELIZABETH smiles in the darkness, then moves over to make room for him. OLIVIER lies down beside her, heaving a blissful sigh. He falls asleep immediately, pressed against her chest. SERGE raises himself abruptly on his elbow.

SERGE: No, not that! We said that's over!
ELIZABETH: Let him go to sleep. I'll carry him to his room later.
SERGE: You're doing more harm than good . . . he's big enough now . . .

The boy presses still more tightly against his mother, who, in accommodating him, jostles her husband. Furious, he sits on the edge of the bed, his head between his hands. He is silent for a moment, and then jumps to his feet, scooping the boy up in his arms. OLIVIER starts to cry. ELIZABETH gets up, raging.

ELIZABETH: Leave him alone!
SERGE: Enough of this fussing! He's a boy, do you understand? Not a little girl, or a bunny, or a fancy pants! I won't let you make him a mama's pet or a faggot!

SERGE carries OLIVIER toward his room.

INT. DUVALS' HOUSE. OLIVIER'S/NADINE'S ROOMS. NIGHT.

SERGE brings OLIVIER to his room and drops him on his bed. The boy continues to sob.

SERGE is on his way back when he hears a whisper.

NADINE: Papa . . .
SERGE (*explodes*): Are you all crazy, or what? Do you know what time it is, Nadine? Go back to sleep! After a whole day's work, I can't even close my eyes . . . You couldn't have a little respect, could you? Not a lot, just a little bit. It's for all of you that I slave, you know . . . You don't realize . . . The shitheads, the bitches, the grannies, it's all for you, not for me . . .

NADINE doesn't answer. SERGE calms down, enters his daughter's room, bends over her bed and gives her a kiss.

SERGE: Okay. Sleep, sleep now. . . . Good night, my beautiful girl . . .

She doesn't respond. Her father walks toward the door and closes it behind him. She bites her lips. There is a light patter of bare feet on the floor. OLIVIER, still clutching his pillow, heads toward his sister's bed and slides under the covers. NADINE makes room for him without protest. The brother and sister fall asleep, pressed against one another.

INT. DUVALS' HOUSE. PARENTS' ROOM. NIGHT.

SERGE, lying on his back, is incapable of closing his eyes.

ELIZABETH: You're not asleep?
SERGE: You win. I won't be able to go back to sleep.
ELIZABETH: Warm up my legs, hmm?

ELIZABETH presses against him, putting her legs between SERGE's thighs; he squeezes and rubs them. She is trembling lightly.

SERGE: You're cold . . .
ELIZABETH: I'm afraid . . .
SERGE: Of what?
ELIZABETH: Today on TV they showed that plane that crashed. All those poor people, their bodies torn to pieces, scattered all around . . . and there were children . . .
SERGE: Calm down. There aren't any pilots in our family. You shouldn't get into these states over every little thing. . . . Go to sleep, now . . .

ELIZABETH is silent. They lie there in the darkness.

INT./EXT. DUVALS' HOUSE. KITCHEN/CHICKEN COOP. DAY.

ELIZABETH is putting the finishing touches on the food basket for the Grandmother. Through the window she sees MARCEL, the neighbor, cutting grass. He stops and flashes her a big smile. She waves "hello."

ELIZABETH looks in the refrigerator for eggs, and finds only two.

ELIZABETH is looking for eggs in the chicken coop. Not finding any, she checks the hens suspiciously. They cackle defiantly.

ELIZABETH: But . . . what's happening to the eggs?

INT. DUVALS' HOUSE. ATTIC. DAY.

On the upper floor of the house, in a well-hidden corner of the attic, among wood chips, boards, rags, broken toys, NADINE, on her knees, is building a pyramid out of the stolen eggs. She dips them in glue and sets them one on top of the other with meticulous care. The structure is already almost two feet high.

From the ground floor, her mother's voice reaches her.

ELIZABETH (*o.s.*): Nadine! Nadine!

NADINE pretends not to hear. She reaches into the basket and pulls out another egg.

ELIZABETH (*o.s.*): Nadine!

No response.

INT. DUVALS' HOUSE. BATHROOM. DAY.

OLIVIER is sitting on the toilet reading some comics. He hears his mother's voice.

ELIZABETH (*o.s.*): Olivier!
OLIVIER: Here I am!
ELIZABETH (*o.s.*): Where are you?
OLIVIER: Here, in the bathroom!

The door of the bathroom opens, and ELIZABETH appears in the doorway.

ELIZABETH: You've been on the pot for at least an hour, haven't you?

OLIVIER assumes a contrite air.

ELIZABETH: You wouldn't know by any chance where Nadine is hiding?
OLIVIER: She's still at Babette's, I bet you.
ELIZABETH: Then you'll have to go to Grandma's. We have to bring her her lunch.

OLIVIER makes a face, pursing his lips.

ELIZABETH: What?
OLIVIER: You know . . .

ELIZABETH has just understood his allusion.

ELIZABETH: It's out of the question! Not at your age!
OLIVIER: Oh, please, Mommy.
ELIZABETH: You know very well what Papa would say if . . .
OLIVIER: But he isn't here.

The two smile conspiratorially.

ELIZABETH: I don't understand why you can't do it by yourself.
OLIVIER: It gives me the creeps, that's all.
ELIZABETH: And what about me?
OLIVIER: But you said yourself that I'm a little delicate.

His mother resigns herself, not knowing how to refuse him anything.

ELIZABETH: But this is absolutely the last time. You'd better swear it!
OLIVIER: I swear it, Mommy! . . . Tell me, do extraterrestrials also make caca?
ELIZABETH: Yes, blue caca.

She bends toward him, wipes his behind with paper, and then, holding her nose, she flushes the toilet. OLIVIER smiles. ELIZABETH pulls up the boy's pants, but her gaze stops at his lower abdomen, where there is a large scar, from a recent appendectomy. She touches the scar gently.

ELIZABETH: Does it still hurt you?
OLIVIER: No. . . .

He stretches out his arms toward his mother and presses against her.

EXT. IN FRONT OF DUVALS' HOUSE. DAY.

OLIVIER, his red cap on his head, is checking a bicycle tire. ELIZABETH waits next to him, the basket of provisions in her hand.

OLIVIER: Mommy, my chain keeps coming off—can I take Nadine's?
ELIZABETH: Of course.
OLIVIER: I have to wait for Papa?
ELIZABETH: Only if you like.

She fastens the basket to the carrier and watches him leave. The small attic window opens and NADINE appears in it.

NADINE (*furiously*): Strictly forbidden! Don't touch my bicycle!

OLIVIER laughs and pedals faster.

NADINE: Olivier! I'll make you pay for this!

EXT. COUNTRY ROAD. DAY.

OLIVIER is riding the bike jubilantly through a field of poppies. His red cap bobs among the tall flowers. He goes by Marcel's house. MARCEL, at his door, straightens up when he sees the boy. He calls him and waves to him.

MARCEL: Olivier! Wait! I have something for you!

OLIVIER brakes slowly, and turns toward the neighbor's house.

INT. DUVALS' HOUSE. LIVING ROOM. LATE AFTERNOON.

Stretched out on the living room sofa, ELIZABETH, her eyes closed, is listening to a Beethoven quartet on the stereo.

INT. DUVALS' HOUSE. NADINE'S ROOM. DUSK.

It's getting dark. NADINE and her friend BABETTE, a little chubby blonde, are seated next to one another. They haven't turned on the lights.

BABETTE: Do you know that Marie-Claire already had her period?
NADINE: Really? . . . I'm not in a hurry, let it be as late as possible.
BABETTE: Mama says that I'll get it soon, too. . . . Look . . .

She raises her T-shirt and proudly displays two budding breasts.

BABETTE: And I also have hair . . . there . . .

She smiles proudly and looks at NADINE *with a certain compassion. She touches* NADINE'S *chest.*

BABETTE: You have hardly anything.

NADINE, somewhat ashamed, pushes her hands away.

NADINE: When you have your period, the blood starts flowing, and you have to wear sanitary napkins and your stomach hurts. I don't see why I should be in a hurry. Papa operates on cats so that they don't ever have it. I'll ask him to operate on me, too.
BABETTE: Have you gone crazy? Later, you couldn't have kids.
NADINE: And who told you that I want to have kids? Do you think I want to be like my mother . . .

Outside, there is a noise of a car pulling up in front of the house. The sound of brakes and a car door closing. Through the window, NADINE sees SERGE, who has returned home.

BABETTE: Your mother is nuts.
NADINE: Yeah, parents are a drag. When Dad starts his big speeches, I just doze off. And Mommy, the only thing that she knows how to do . . . (*lowering her voice*) . . . you promise not to tell anyone?
BABETTE: I promise.
NADINE: She comes into Olivier's room at night and she licks him like a cow.

BABETTE laughs.

NADINE: If it was up to me, my brother never would have been born.

INT./EXT. DUVALS' HOUSE. SERGE'S OFFICE. LIVING ROOM. EARLY EVENING.

SERGE opens the front door, looking angry and bitter. A WOMAN, the wife of the café owner, is in the waiting room, with an enormous CAT on her lap.

The veterinarian's arrival startles the animal, which tries to escape. SERGE shakes his head, takes off his coat and heads immediately toward his office, propelling the WOMAN before him.

Piano music is coming from the living room.

SERGE puts the CAT on the table; the animal calms down under his firm grip.

SERGE: Have you taken his temperature?
WOMAN: He never lets me do that!

SERGE inserts a thermometer in the CAT's anus. He still looks furious. He sees ELIZABETH, who is standing motionless in the doorway to the office, her hair in disarray and her expression vague, as if she were asleep on her feet.

ELIZABETH: You're already back?

SERGE glares at her angrily.

SERGE: This time, you've crossed the line! Leaving a sick old woman all day without food! You're really a slut, or else completely wacko.

ELIZABETH stands with her mouth gaping. She stares at her husband, bewildered.

ELIZABETH: What are you talking about, all day without food?

Meanwhile, SERGE has given the CAT an injection, and the syringe is still stuck in its thigh. At Elizabeth's last question, he straightens up and stares at her: her astonishment is such that he immediately becomes acutely uneasy.

At that moment, the girls come down the stairs. BABETTE smiles, but NADINE, who has heard her mother's last words and notices the fear in her voice, motions to BABETTE to be quiet.

ELIZABETH stares at SERGE, perplexed.
ELIZABETH: Olivier? Where is Olivier?
SERGE: Olivier?
ELIZABETH: You didn't bring him?
SERGE: Where was I supposed to bring him from?
ELIZABETH: He went to your mother's . . . with a basket of . . .
SERGE: About what time?
ELIZABETH: Early in the afternoon, about one o'clock. . . . (*Pale and trembling*) She hasn't seen him all day?
SERGE: No.

SERGE suddenly releases the CAT that he is still holding, and the animal, with the syringe still embedded in its hip, charges through the room, yowling. The WOMAN tries in vain to catch him. While this is happening, SERGE and ELIZABETH are talking at once, extremely agitated.

ELIZABETH: He's disappeared! He won't come back! . . .
SERGE: Calm down! He must have gone to Jacques' house . . .
ELIZABETH: No! Jacques already phoned and wanted to talk to him. . . . I knew it . . .
SERGE: He's with somebody else. . . . Get hold of yourself, look . . .
ELIZABETH: I knew it!

NADINE looks back and forth between her father and mother. BABETTE, disturbed by the scene, starts to walk toward the door.

NADINE (*to Babette*): No! Wait!
BABETTE: But I have to go. My mother told me to come back before the news. I have to watch little Paul.
SERGE: Elizabeth, just try to think where he could have . . .

But ELIZABETH is not listening to him anymore. She rushes past him and runs outside.

EXT. OUTSIDE DUVALS' HOUSE/THE FIELDS. EARLY EVENING.

ELIZABETH, in a hallucinatory state, beside herself, runs in front of the house and further, into the fields.

ELIZABETH: Olivier! Olivier!

Her cries reverberate in the silent landscape.

INT. DUVALS' HOUSE. SERGE'S OFFICE. EARLY EVENING.

The CAT is still running wild in the office, making a terrible mess, knocking over vials and instruments. SERGE finally grabs it; with a precise gesture, he withdraws the needle from its thigh and tosses the CAT to the WOMAN. SERGE runs to the telephone and dials rapidly.

SERGE: Mama? Olivier never came to your house today, did he? Yes, she sent him with your lunch! Around noon! I don't know where he went. If I knew it, I wouldn't be phoning you! Leave me alone, for God's sake. Don't add your shit to everything else! . . . Excuse me . . .

He hangs up in a rage. Turning around, he encounters the curious gaze of the WOMAN, who stares at him with the CAT held tightly in her arms. NADINE is behind her, clutching BABETTE's arm convulsively. SERGE motions to her to go to her room.

From outside, ELIZABETH's desperate cries are echoing.

ELIZABETH (*o.s.*): Olivier! My little lamb!

EXT. FOREST. NIGHT.

The deep blackness of the forest is pierced by lantern light. Barking of dogs, men calling, the intermittent sound of gongs beaten by the searchers.

VOICES: Olivier! Olivier!

POLICEMEN, VILLAGERS with dogs, MARCEL, SERGE, his face pale and tense. Suddenly, from the edge of the forest, a cry is heard.

VOICES: This way! Come over here!

They all come running.

Near the road, a YOUNG MAN is leaning over a bicycle, which lies backwards on the ground. Everyone surrounds it closely.

The YOUNG MAN raises his eyes to SERGE:

YOUNG MAN: It's his bicycle, isn't it?
SERGE: It's quite possible . . .

DRUOT, a young policeman with a strong build and a mustache, has just noticed an object lying several feet from the bicycle. He aims his flashlight, quickly finding Olivier's red cap.

INT. DUVALS' HOUSE. LIVING ROOM/KITCHEN. DAWN.

NEIGHBORS wander between the kitchen and the living room. ELIZABETH is seated, collapsed, on the sofa. A NEIGHBOR holds her hand and comforts her.

Inspector DRUOT has spread out a pile of papers on the living room table. With other POLICE OFFICERS, he is busy writing up the proceedings. He is questioning MARCEL.

MARCEL: About one o'clock, I guess. The kid was riding his bike near my house . . .
DRUOT: At what distance, approximately?
MARCEL: Something like thirty feet. . . . I was out of smokes, so I called for him to bring me two packs. I gave him ten francs. With the rest, he could buy himself some candy. He said okay and he left, that's all that . . .

He raises his eyes toward SERGE, who is pacing nervously from one corner of the living room to another.

A fat NEIGHBOR offers SERGE a cup of coffee.

NEIGHBOR: Drink up, Mr. Duval.
SERGE: All right.

He grabs the cup, but sets it down immediately, without bringing it to his lips. He leaves the room, followed by the curious gaze of the NEIGHBORS, and goes up to the bedrooms.

DRUOT turns to ELIZABETH.

DRUOT: Do you know of anything that would have made the boy run away?

ELIZABETH stares at him, not understanding his question.

DRUOT: Had he been beaten? Was he afraid of something? Had he done anything stupid?

She shakes her head without saying a word.

INT. DUVALS' HOUSE. NADINE'S ROOM. DAWN.

SERGE is seated on NADINE's bed. He is holding his daughter's hand; she appears withdrawn and defiant, like a frightened animal. ELIZABETH's piercing cry reaches them.

INT. DUVALS' HOUSE. LIVING ROOM. DAWN.

ELIZABETH is screaming, her head thrown back. SERGE brings an ampoule out of his office and gives an injection to ELIZABETH, who is held up by a NEIGHBOR. MARCEL and DRUOT watch the scene.

ELIZABETH: He was all that I had . . .

She clutches at the inspector, shakes him, and screams.

ELIZABETH: You're going to find him. . . . Swear to me . . . swear to me. . . . He's the only one I have, do you understand?
DRUOT (*solemnly*): I swear to you, Madame.

INT. DUVALS' HOUSE. ATTIC. DAWN.

NADINE lights the candles. The egg pyramid gleams in the wavering light.

NADINE (*whispers*): Let them find him . . . make them find him.

She goes to the structure and methodically breaks one egg after another. After a while, the floor is covered with the white and yellow of eggs.

NADINE wipes her dirty hands on her nightgown. She takes a cigarette from a hiding place, lights it from a candle, and presses the burning cigarette to her left breast. She grimaces in pain, but keeps pressing.

NADINE (*whispering*): Let them find him . . .

EXT. IN FRONT OF GRANDMOTHER'S HOUSE. DAY.

NADINE comes out of her grandmother's house with a schoolbag on her back. The OLD LADY moves with difficulty, but all the same, she walks her granddaughter to the doorway.

OLD LADY: I asked your father not to send you by yourself.

NADINE: Babette is with me.

She gestures toward the other side of the road, where BABETTE is waiting with the two bicycles.

OLD LADY: And your mother, how is she?

NADINE lowers her head and looks at her grandmother from the corners of her eyes.

NADINE: She's okay.
OLD LADY: She says it's because of me, doesn't she?
NADINE (*hesitates before lying*): No.
OLD LADY: And the police? What do the police say?
NADINE: Nothing. They've been going around in circles for three weeks.

The OLD LADY sighs deeply. She presses her lips to her granddaughter's cheeks. NADINE tries to conceal her distaste for that wet kiss.

OLD LADY: If they would at least find the body, we could bury it properly.
NADINE (*protesting*): Grandma!

Now the OLD LADY has tears in her eyes. NADINE is somewhat moved.

OLD LADY: You know, she's dead.
NADINE: Who?
OLD LADY: My dog.

NADINE blushes. She goes down the steps rapidly, and, without looking back, runs toward BABETTE, who is waiting at the entrance with her bicycle.

In silence, the OLD LADY watches the two girls ride away, raising a cloud of dust as they go. A few fragments of their conversation are heard:

BABETTE: Did you see the film on channel 2?
NADINE: Terrific, wasn't it?

INT. DUVALS' HOUSE. LIVING ROOM/KITCHEN. EVENING.

NADINE is watching television—the evening news.

ELIZABETH (*o.s.*): Nadine! Dinner is ready.

INT. DUVALS' HOUSE. KITCHEN. EVENING.

NADINE enters the room and sits at the table, around which are four chairs, as usual. SERGE is already seated, his face hidden by a newspaper. ELIZABETH serves macaroni, on her face a look of cold estrangement. She serves NADINE a piece of meat, before sitting down herself. SERGE folds his newspaper, and then begins to eat. From time to time, he looks at his daughter and smiles at her. NADINE eats with a healthy appetite.

ELIZABETH picks at the macaroni with her fork, then pushes her plate away. She looks silently at her husband and daughter, who continue to eat.

SERGE: Elizabeth. . . . You can't go on like this. You have to eat something.
ELIZABETH: I'll do what I want.
SERGE: Fine. . . . As you like . . .

SERGE and NADINE eat in silence. ELIZABETH gets up from the table, takes her plate, and dumps it in the sink with a gesture of distaste. She sits down again, pours herself a full glass of wine, and drinks it in gulps.

SERGE (*in an artificially detached tone*): Jean-Pierre phoned me today. . . . He told me that they're looking for veterinarians for Chad . . . a two-year contract . . . for the moment.

NADINE suddenly brightens up.

NADINE: Chad. It's in Africa, isn't it?
SERGE: In Black Africa.
NADINE: Fantastic! Could we really go there?
SERGE: I put in my application . . . very interesting work . . . something different from this routine.
ELIZABETH (*indifferently*): And your mother? Will you pack her in your luggage?

SERGE: She'll be a lot better off in the retirement home. She finally understands that . . . it took some time . . .
ELIZABETH: If only she had decided earlier . . .
SERGE: Elizabeth . . . I'm begging you . . .

ELIZABETH gets up and leaves the kitchen. SERGE and NADINE eat without looking at one another. ELIZABETH reappears in the doorway, her eyes red.

ELIZABETH: Go away from here? What if he comes back and doesn't find anybody?

SERGE doesn't respond.

ELIZABETH (*screaming*): You've drawn a line, huh? As if he didn't exist anymore! As if it were over!

SERGE gets up also. He is shaking.

SERGE (*quietly and tensely*): Shut up! He's my son, too, you know!

ELIZABETH leaves. SERGE sighs deeply. He leans his forehead against the door frame. NADINE regards him silently. He notices her gaze and smiles at her weakly.

INT. DUVALS' HOUSE. NADINE'S ROOM. NIGHT.

NADINE is getting undressed. Naked, she approaches the window, and looks at her reflection in the glass. Her breasts are already slightly contoured. She touches the bandage below her left nipple. She reacts when she hears footsteps in the next room—her brother's—the door to which is closed now. She quickly puts on her nightgown and slides under the sheets. She strains to hear the muffled voice of her mother—who appears to be singing.

NADINE gets up and walks softly toward the door. The voice becomes silent. The door opens wide, revealing ELIZABETH. She looks at her daughter furiously, almost with hatred.

ELIZABETH: Nadine!

The girl pulls back.

ELIZABETH: You touched Olivier's things!
NADINE: I didn't . . .

ELIZABETH cuts short her attempt to explain. She grabs her by the arms and shakes her vigorously.

ELIZABETH: Don't lie! Don't lie!
NADINE (*sobbing*): I only took his marker . . . only a marker. . . . I needed it. For school . . .
ELIZABETH: Dirty, selfish girl! Liar!
NADINE: Please, Mommy . . .

She cries more and more desperately.

ELIZABETH is beside herself, in a full-blown fit of fury. There is something monstrous in her attack on her daughter. Holding Nadine to the floor, she shakes her violently.

ELIZABETH: If you had gone there yourself, instead of hiding in the attic, he would still be with us! You know it!
NADINE: But I couldn't know. . . . How. . . . It's not my fault.
ELIZABETH: It really *is* your fault, do you understand? *Yours* . . .

ELIZABETH kicks her hard.

NADINE: No, Mama. . . . Please . . .
ELIZABETH: Yours! And your father's! And all of you . . .

Alerted by their screaming and crying, SERGE bursts into the room and throws himself on ELIZABETH. He seizes her by the wrists, freeing NADINE.

SERGE: You're completely crazy! Leave the kid alone!

SERGE wants to embrace NADINE, but she pushes him away and turns to her mother . . .

NADINE: I didn't want it to happen, Mama, I didn't want it.
SERGE: Crazy bitch, cut it out! You see what you've driven her to? You don't have any right . . .

ELIZABETH: If it wasn't for your stupid bitch of a mother. . . . If Nadine had done what I told her to . . .
SERGE: You'd rather it happened to her than to him?
ELIZABETH: Yes, I would have preferred it, do you hear me?
NADINE: Mama!

SERGE takes his head in his hands. He paces back and forth in the room.

SERGE (*moaning*): I can't take this! I'm not putting up with this much longer! If you had only moved your own ass for once, to take that damned basket . . .

ELIZABETH leaves NADINE crying, and turns to her husband.

ELIZABETH: I hate you! You're just a nothing . . . a failure . . . an impotent little veterinarian. You're suffocating me, you understand? My whole life. . . . I put up with it only because I had Olivier . . .

SERGE blushes. He slaps her face hard. NADINE, frightened, seizes her father's wrists, trying to hold him back. He pushes her away roughly.

SERGE: I've had enough! Now you won't have to put up with me anymore!

He turns his back and leaves.

ELIZABETH has trouble catching her breath. NADINE has stopped crying. Crouched in a corner, she sucks the blood which is flowing from the palm of her hand. ELIZABETH walks haltingly in her direction. NADINE withdraws deeper into her corner. ELIZABETH kneels before her and takes her hand gently, stopping the flow of blood.

ELIZABETH: Did you cut yourself?

She draws NADINE toward her and hugs her. The girl at first defiantly resists her mother's caresses. ELIZABETH starts to rock her like a baby, with tears in her eyes.

ELIZABETH (*whispers*): My little girl. . . . Forgive me, can't you? My dear little girl . . .

INT. DUVALS' HOUSE. PARENTS' BEDROOM. NIGHT.

In the darkness of the room, SERGE feels his way into bed. He slides under the covers, without touching ELIZABETH, who is stretched out by his side. But she reaches her hand toward him. He pushes her away.

SERGE: Leave me alone.

She presses against him, and leaning on her elbows, tries again to arouse him. He pulls away, but she insistently leans on him. She is breathing hard. They wrestle in the darkness. Finally, ELIZABETH climbs on top of SERGE, who, against his will, feels the beginning of an erection. He stays motionless on his back while ELIZABETH again takes the initiative. She makes love to him. She whispers unconsciously.

ELIZABETH: Give it to me. . . . Give me the child . . .

The first light of dawn can be seen through the windows.

INT. DUVALS' HOUSE. NADINE'S ROOM. DAWN.

NADINE shudders in her sleep and wakes up with a start as if affected by a noise coming from her parents' room. She jumps briskly from bed, pulls on her boots, and puts her rain cape on over her nightgown. Noiselessly, she hurries down the stairs.

EXT. FIELD/FOREST. DAWN

NADINE runs across the field. She stumbles, falls, and resumes her course.

In the forest, she crawls on her stomach in the trench where she and Olivier played.

NADINE (*urgently*): Olivier! Olivier! Come out. I know you're there. The game's over, Olivier, come back!

There is no response. NADINE is motionless, straining her ears. Suddenly, she hears the snap of branches and twigs breaking underfoot. She raises herself out of the trench and looks through the tangled grass: she sees a herd of COWS at the edge of the woods. Heavy, dark masses, they shake their heads and moo in the semidarkness.

INT. DUVALS' HOUSE. SERGE'S OFFICE. DAY.

Two enormous leather suitcases rest on the floor. SERGE is emptying the shelves methodically, packing his things. He picks up the family photos displayed on the desk: Elizabeth with the children, himself with Nadine. He hesitates, and then puts the photos back in their place.

EXT. OUTSIDE OF DUVALS' HOUSE. DAY.

ELIZABETH returns from feeding the chickens. In front of the house, she suddenly stops. Her arms crossed, absently, she looks at MARCEL, who is mowing hay in the meadow opposite.

EXT. GRANDMOTHER'S HOUSE/THE ROAD. DAY.

SERGE fastens a padlock on the door of his mother's house. The OLD LADY is already waiting for him by the car.

SERGE loads the last of her possessions into the trunk. He helps her into the front seat and starts the car.

He is driving down the road that goes through the fields. The OLD LADY gazes into the distance directly before her, without saying a word or looking back.

EXT. IN FRONT OF THE VILLAGE SCHOOL. DAY.

SERGE parks his car in front of the school. The KIDS are jostling noisily at the door, chasing one another.

SERGE catches sight of NADINE, who comes out with BABETTE and some other GIRLS. They are smiling and chattering animatedly.

Seeing her father, NADINE turns serious and walks slowly toward the car. She looks up at him as he hugs her.

NADINE: Did something happen?
SERGE: No. I wanted to talk with you a little, that's all. Want some ice cream?

NADINE shrugs her shoulders.

INT. VILLAGE CAFÉ. DAY.

SERGE and NADINE are seated opposite one another. Some YOUNG PEOPLE are drinking wine and joking with the WAITRESS. An enormous portion of half-melted ice cream is sitting in front of NADINE.

SERGE: Don't think that I'm trying to run away from you all.

NADINE doesn't react. She stirs the half-melted ice cream with her spoon.

SERGE: Look at me.

She raises her eyes briefly toward him and lowers them immediately.

SERGE: I've decided that it's better this way. . . . I just can't . . . I can't take it any longer. You'll understand later . . .
NADINE: Oh, yes . . . and what's there to understand?
SERGE: That it will be better this way, for all of us, believe me.

NADINE remains silent. She sets her spoon down on the dish, and the melted ice cream drips onto the table.

SERGE: And now . . . you do what you want. When I'm settled down, you can follow me there . . . live with me . . . a great life, huh?

She doesn't react.

SERGE: Would you rather stay here with your mother?

NADINE still doesn't respond. In the melted ice cream on the table, she traces some letters, forming a mysterious abbreviation: I.H.Y.B.

SERGE observes her actions.

SERGE: What does that mean?

NADINE, startled, lifts her head.

SERGE: What have you written?

She doesn't answer. Father and daughter eye one another.

SERGE: "I hate you, bastard!" Is that it?

NADINE blushes. With her spoon, she obliterates the letters. SERGE reaches out his hand toward his daughter, jostling her arm. She withdraws instinctively. Finally, she looks at him again.

NADINE (*measuring her words*): You don't love us, really. You never loved us . . .
SERGE: You know very well that's not true . . .
NADINE: You don't love Mom.
SERGE: I did everything I could. I plowed through the whole region, I knocked at every door. I did all the newspapers, radio, television. . . . What more could I have done? . . . We absolutely have to . . . try to turn the page. . . . Alone, I mean, each one for himself. Later on . . . later on, we'll see. Do you understand?
NADINE: No!
SERGE: You have to understand!

NADINE is still silent.

SERGE: Shit, this isn't a confessional! . . . As if I had to justify myself!

He gets up. He talks so loudly now that the café CUSTOMERS turn in his direction.

SERGE: Look where you've pushed me, you and your mother! I'm going to take care of myself. You won't get me this way . . .

NADINE observes his anger and can't help smiling. SERGE looks around the room, calms down, and takes his seat again. She continues to smile. She pats his hand gently.

NADINE: Poor Papa . . .

SERGE stares at NADINE.

NADINE (*gently but firmly*): I'll stay with Mama.

EXT. DUVALS' HOUSE. YARD. DAY.

MARCEL and ELIZABETH are working in the garden. MARCEL is cleaning the pond. She is throwing old furniture in a pile. Inspector DRUOT is coming down the road.

Upon catching sight of him, ELIZABETH freezes. She waits for him to approach. MARCEL also stops working; he watches the inspector. DRUOT can hardly stand ELIZABETH's questioning gaze as he gives her his hand.

DRUOT: I've come to say goodbye, Madame. I'm being transferred to Paris.

She doesn't answer. She brings the can of gasoline near the pile of furniture, pours it on and lights the fire. The flames shoot up. MARCEL takes a few steps toward them. He stops and watches the fire.

ELIZABETH: I've wanted to get rid of this stuff for a long time. The dust. . . . It's all full of dust.

Through the open window, we see the nearly empty living room, and the white walls that NADINE is painting.

ELIZABETH: Marcel is a big help to us. It's too much for me . . . the garden . . . the pond . . . the children always wanted to stock it with fish. But Serge never had the time.

DRUOT glances at MARCEL: the young man makes him uncomfortable.

DRUOT: I wanted to tell you that I've done everything I possibly could . . .
ELIZABETH: So, you're abandoning us . . .
DRUOT: I'm not abandoning Olivier, I give you my word. But . . .

He doesn't finish. ELIZABETH suddenly begins to smile.

ELIZABETH (*without looking at the inspector*): Do you know that Olivier came into the world twice?

DRUOT swallows. He looks at MARCEL, who is leaning on his rake.

ELIZABETH: We didn't have any trouble when Nadine was born. But Olivier was born in the seventh month. They laid him on my stomach . . . so pink, so cute already. . . . I wanted to take him in my arms, but suddenly, he started to turn blue, then purple . . . his little feet and his hands, then all of him, right up to his face. . . . Serge shouted for help...he understood what was happening. They took the baby away from me immediately. They told me he was being revived. I was in a complete panic. "My son, where is my baby?" I asked. Serge held my hand and kept saying it's okay, normal. . . . "They're bathing him now . . . " Half an hour later the nurse came back. . . . She said, "He's out of danger now. He's going to live!" And Serge . . . (*she laughs*) Serge fainted! From joy! Can you imagine? He's a doctor . . . well, a veterinarian, it's the same thing! . . . And he fainted! . . .

ELIZABETH smiles through her tears. DRUOT lowers his eyes. She turns, takes a few steps in Marcel's direction, and suddenly collapses on the ground. DRUOT rushes toward her. MARCEL kneels beside her and leans over her face, a glimmer of distress in his eyes. He mutters something, his lips trembling, and leans over Elizabeth's face, as if he wanted to kiss her. He raises his eyes to the inspector.

NADINE comes out of the house, smeared with paint. She runs toward her mother and gets down on her knees next to her. Without emotion, as if accustomed to these incidents, she unbuttons her mother's blouse, and unfastens her bra, while slapping her cheeks briskly. ELIZABETH gradually regains consciousness. NADINE helps her up.

NADINE: Come in, come in, or you'll catch cold . . .

DRUOT wants to assist her, but she gestures for him to leave and leads ELIZABETH toward the house.

MARCEL stares at them. He then takes his rake and, without paying any attention to DRUOT, walks back toward the pond.

It is almost dark. The fire is still blazing. DRUOT watches the woman walk away with a faltering step, supported by the girl. He is deeply moved.

DRUOT (*whispers*): I've sworn to you that I won't abandon you.

INT. DUVALS' HOUSE. PARENTS' ROOM. DAY.

NADINE helps ELIZABETH to the double bed. She lies down at her side, and gently caresses her mother's shoulders and back. ELIZABETH breathes shallowly, keeping her eyes closed.

NADINE (*whispers*): Shh. . . . I'm here.

ELIZABETH opens her eyes. She looks at NADINE.

ELIZABETH (*with a lump in her throat*): It's already so cold, and Olivier is wearing only a T-shirt.

NADINE falls silent, abruptly ceasing her caresses. They remain stretched out side by side, immobile.

EXT. STREET IN PARIS. NIGHT.

A band of HOODLUMS occupy the sidewalk, harassing the PASSERS-BY. *They surround an OLD MAN, pushing him against a back door. One blond BOY more composed and commanding than the rest, takes a knife out of his pocket and robs the OLD MAN. The BOY runs away. A police car appears, its siren wailing. The BOY runs down the steps of the subway entrance.*

INT. SUBWAY STATION. NIGHT.

There are several late PASSENGERS *on the platform. A dirty WOMAN moans in a monotone. Dirty wrappers and old newspapers are strewn all about.*

The BOY hears the noise of the arriving train. He runs faster, preparing to jump over the turnstile, and lands right in the arms of a POLICEMAN, who has run over from the platform. He turns around, hoping to flee in the opposite direction, but there he sees the fat plainclothes POLICE-MAN. The BOY stops and smiles at the fat man.

BOY: So. A guy can't have a good time in peace anymore? The neighborhood is off limits to people under eighteen, is that it?

The FAT POLICEMAN in plain clothes and the UNIFORMED POLICEMAN lead him toward the exit. The WOMAN continues to moan.

INT. POLICE STATION IN PARIS. INSPECTOR SIMARD'S OFFICE. NIGHT.

Chief Inspector SIMARD, about 50 years of age, appears tired. The POLICEMAN who took part in the arrest is leaning against the wall, behind the inspector.

The BOY is seated respectfully on a chair facing the inspector, and is responding to his questions like a docile pupil.

BOY (*sincerely*): . . . I arrived less than a week ago . . . to find my Mom . . . she's a Baltic princess . . . the Emir of Kuwait took her to Paris and dropped her, then she was working as a housekeeper at the Swedish Embassy, her father was Scandinavian, you know . . .
SIMARD: We'll check your mother's name . . .
BOY: Greta Garbo.

The POLICEMAN bursts out laughing. The BOY continues, unperturbed.

BOY: My father was the king of Kiwi, an Egyptian Jew by origin; Alexandria, you know, Inspector. He died in the attack on the train to Marseilles. They found him all squashed, a bomb, you know. I got out of there by a miracle . . .
SIMARD (*interrupting*): His name was Rockefeller, huh? You're probably not even fifteen . . .

The BOY smiles at him seductively.

BOY: Why? Am I already too old for you?

SIMARD has had enough of the teenager's fantasies. He turns toward the POLICEMAN:

SIMARD: This guy of ours is an ace at make-believe, isn't he? He should have been an actor.

The BOY interrupts him and begins to recite a new tale.

BOY: Okay, I'll tell you everything. No fooling, this time. My name is Sebastian Blanch. My stepfather took me by force the first time in our bathroom at home, while my mother was out. . . . Since then, I've had a fixation with public toilets.

The POLICEMAN gets up and moves toward the BOY, as if he intends to strike him. SIMARD shouts, and stops his colleague with a gesture.

The door opens to reveal inspector DRUOT, carrying the files of children who have disappeared. Inspector SIMARD, his boss, starts shuffling through the documents, his gaze shifting between the identity photos and the BOY.

SIMARD: He isn't in there. What can we do with the little shit? Why don't you adopt him, Druot, a bachelor like you?

The BOY turns toward DRUOT. His cheeks are puffed out; he is playing the little boy, taking a red baseball cap out of his pocket and shoving it on his head.

BOY: Hello, Daddy . . .
DRUOT: Where do I know you from, anyway?
BOY: Maybe from the pilgrimage to Chartres . . . with the Scouts.

DRUOT looks at the BOY intensely, struggling to remember something. Suddenly, as if inspired, he turns toward SIMARD.

DRUOT: Boss, do you remember when I was transferred to Paris, approximately?

SIMARD is about to answer him, but DRUOT turns around and exits quickly.

SIMARD (*to the POLICEMAN*): Our national Columbo is on the trail again!

INT. POLICE STATION. DRUOT'S OFFICE. NIGHT.

DRUOT has taken all of the files out of the cabinet. He shuffles through them, raising clouds of dust.

At last he finds it; triumphantly, he pulls out an old file: "1984, Olivier Duval." His hands tremble with excitement.

The door opens—a POLICEMAN comes in, leading a big fellow, MICKY.

MICKY (*shouts, struggling*): Bastards! Let me go! You've made a big mistake. . . . You took me for somebody else! You're going to pay for this. . . . I'm telling you . . .

DRUOT doesn't even glance at him. In a state of great excitement, he looks at a photo. It shows a smiling little boy in the arms of a blond young woman whose eyes are filled with tenderness.

INT. POLICE STATION. CORRIDOR NEXT TO CELLS/A CELL. NIGHT.

Everyone is asleep in the cells. The BOY is also sleeping. He is stretched out on his back on the cot, his eyes closed, his fists clenched. The dim light from the hall illuminates him through the bars.

A GUARD is seated at the end of the corridor, Walkman headphones on his ears, an English manual open on his lap.

GUARD: "I want. . . . You want . . ."

DRUOT and SIMARD arrive silently from the office side. DRUOT is holding little Olivier's file open in his hand. He stops before the BOY's cell. Through the bars, he observes his peaceful face.

DRUOT looks anxiously at SIMARD, who is comparing the BOY's face to the photograph.

SIMARD (*skeptically*): How would I know?

DRUOT, excited, interrupts him.

DRUOT: I'm very sure, boss! It was my first case. I'd give my right arm. . . . If the parents identify him. . . . Here . . . listen to this.

He unfolds a newspaper clipping.

DRUOT (*reads*): "There is still no news of little Olivier Duval, who disappeared on August 10, 1984. The investigation has turned up nothing. His parents, Elizabeth and Serge Duval—the father is a veterinarian, the couple have a second child, Nadine, a girl of twelve—are still hoping that the child is alive . . . " He was never found. And now, this kid. . . I tell you, boss, he's the spitting image, I swear to you! Just think what it will mean to these people if it's him.
SIMARD: And if it isn't him?
DRUOT: I'd bet a million that it is, boss.

In the cell, the BOY opens his eyes. It is apparent that he was only pretending to be asleep. He slowly approaches the bars on the door and begins to shake them.

BOY: Let me out!

SIMARD is already in the corridor. DRUOT has stopped. He is listening. The BOY shouts louder and louder. At last the GUARD hears him. He takes off his headphones.

GUARD (*shouts*): Silence in there!

No effect. With all his strength, the BOY bangs his head against the bars. The GUARD runs to give him a nasty punch in the stomach through the bars. The BOY doubles over and falls to the floor.

DRUOT approaches the cell door slowly, and the GUARD notices him at the last moment. He is embarrassed to have a witness to his brutality. Without saying a word, DRUOT takes the key to the cell, opens the door, and enters. The BOY gets up slowly, approaches the little window, and begins to bounce in place like a boxer, as if he were fighting with a shadow. DRUOT observes him silently. He sits on the edge of the cot. After a moment, the BOY looks around. He regards his visitor.

BOY: What are you going to do with me?

DRUOT: That depends on you.

The BOY smiles sarcastically.

DRUOT: Anyone can do a dumb thing in his life . . . especially when he's a kid. . . . You know, I think your parents will be happy that you're alive. You should go back home.
BOY (*surprised*): How do you know?
DRUOT: You learn a few things in a career. Your mother is a terrific woman. She didn't deserve everything you put her through . . .

The BOY looks thoughtful.

DRUOT: Why did you run away, back then?
BOY (*reflecting*): I don't remember.
DRUOT: So, you see . . .

Suddenly, the BOY makes up his mind.

BOY: And if I admit who I am, and so on, will you let me go?
DRUOT: I'll personally hand you over to your mother.

The BOY is silent. His face shows astonishment and dismay. DRUOT touches the BOY's head gently.

DRUOT: You're Olivier, aren't you?

The BOY abruptly raises his head, and gives the inspector a suddenly nostalgic look.

BOY: It's been a long time since anybody called me that.

All at once, DRUOT is seized by doubt. He looks at the BOY cautiously. The latter begins to smile, as if the tension had lifted.

DRUOT: Olivier what?
BOY: What is this? Another interrogation?
DRUOT: Olivier, and then what?
BOY: You know very well! Olivier Duval. . . . My father's name is Serge, he's a veterinarian. My mom's Elizabeth . . . and I have a sister, Nadine . . . she must be . . . 18 years old, I guess. Well? Am I right or not?

The inspector takes the BOY by the shoulders; it seems that he wants to embrace him. He is very moved; his chin is trembling with emotion. The BOY disengages himself roughly. He jumps away, grimacing unpleasantly.

BOY: Hey, cop! You're not part of the family!

INT. POLICE HEADQUARTERS. HALLWAY. DAY.

Inspector DRUOT is leading ELIZABETH, older, changed by the years, through the hallway. Curious SPECTATORS are looking from every door. But ELIZABETH doesn't notice them. She is dressed elegantly compared to her usual attire, wearing shoes with heels that are too high; her makeup is smeared. She doesn't take her eyes off DRUOT.

DRUOT: I don't see how it could not be him. . . . Everything fits; he remembers dates, names . . . the resemblance is striking. If you have doubts, Madame . . . we can try to get him to talk more, we can do new tests . . .
ELIZABETH: You must be joking. If it's him, I'll recognize him at once. I'll know it . . .
DRUOT: Of course, you'll have some problems with him, but with patience and love. . . . In any case, don't worry, he's lucky . . . he's not HIV positive.
ELIZABETH (*interrupting*): Has he grown? How tall is he?
DRUOT: Well, he's a little taller than you.
ELIZABETH: My God! Has he told you . . . why . . .
DRUOT: I advise you not to question him too soon. His nerves are raw . . . he's a little wild.

DRUOT stops in front of a closed door.

DRUOT: Here he is.

ELIZABETH is trembling. She casts a beseeching glance at DRUOT.

ELIZABETH: How do I look?

DRUOT doesn't know how to respond. ELIZABETH rummages in her handbag; everything falls from her hand: keys, change-purse and papers fall to the floor. She bends over to pick them up. Embarrassed, DRUOT helps her; finally, she takes out a tube of lipstick, powder, and a mirror. She puts the open handbag in DRUOT's arms and quickly redoes her makeup. She checks her hair, looks at DRUOT one more time, moves her lips faintly as if saying a prayer; she opens the door and enters.

INT. POLICE HEADQUARTERS. ANTEROOM. DAY.

ELIZABETH and DRUOT enter the anteroom, which has a small window into another room—vast, completely empty, with bars on the window. OLIVIER is alone. He is unaware that someone is watching him—he jumps, crouches, stretches his legs in the air—carrying on imaginary combat with a shadow.

ELIZABETH is glued to the little window. She clenches her fists with all her strength. She doesn't take her eyes off the boy. DRUOT is watching her tensely and nervously.

Suddenly, she rests her hands on the door and calls softly, but with a desperate intensity:

ELIZABETH: Olivier!

He turns his face toward the door, where ELIZABETH is watching. Their eyes meet. OLIVIER smiles gaily; he is beaming.

Relief and emotion are fighting in DRUOT's face. SIMARD appears behind him. DRUOT turns toward him; through his tears his face is triumphant.

DRUOT: I guess I've won that million.

INT. TRAIN COMPARTMENT. SUNSET.

Through the window—the majestic landscape of the French countryside. OLIVIER is alone in the compartment; he is asleep. His head is rocking to the rhythm of the train's motion. The door opens. ELIZABETH, her arms loaded with food and bottles, tries to close the door; she drops some of her things on the seat and picks up the rest. She talks to the boy without noticing that he doesn't hear her.

ELIZABETH: Is this what you like? Anyway, it's what you used to like. Don't be vexed with me, I bought a bit too much so you can choose . . .

Feverishly, she places the different packages on the seat while reading the labels.

ELIZABETH: Rye bread . . . some cheese . . . I got them to add some strong mustard, it's okay, isn't it? Or perhaps you're only thirsty. . . . Look what mother has bought . . . some Coke . . . Nadine is crazy about it . . . it's her drug, she always overdoes things, you won't recognize her, she's become even more eccentric. . . . You'll see when we get home. Here, some lemonade, a ham sandwich . . .

She looks at OLIVIER and realizes, finally, that he is asleep, uncomfortably curled up in the corner of the compartment. She puts down the packages and sits down silently beside him. Then she bends over to gently remove his shoes. She freezes when he stirs, but seeing that he is still asleep, she goes ahead.

ELIZABETH straightens out his legs, and rests them gently on the opposite seat. She touches him somewhat timidly, but when OLIVIER moves, she withdraws her hands as if she were afraid of being caught. She takes off her coat and covers the boy's feet. Then, seated upright, she opens a bottle of wine and drinks it down, without taking her eyes off the boy.

ELIZABETH: You're going to forgive me, aren't you? From now on everything will be normal. . . . I'll do my best . . . a normal home. A real home . . . a real life . . .

She starts making childish, magical gestures with her fingers.

ELIZABETH: "Wooden cross, iron cross. If I lie I go to hell."

The CONDUCTOR opens the door. ELIZABETH makes a panicky gesture, as if to stop him.

CONDUCTOR: Tickets, please.
ELIZABETH: Quiet! Don't you see that he's asleep?

She takes the tickets out of her bag and gives them to him. While he punches them, she drinks again, straight from the bottle, and smiles at him.

ELIZABETH: It's nerves . . . do you understand? . . . Do you have children?
CONDUCTOR: Four.

ELIZABETH takes some chocolates and some drinks and gives them to the CONDUCTOR. He doesn't know how to react, but accepts the gift from this strange woman.

ELIZABETH readjusts the coat over the boy's feet, rests her head on the back of the seat, and falls asleep. The empty bottle falls from her hands and rolls on the floor.

OLIVIER wakes up and opens his eyes. He looks at the sleeping ELIZABETH, reflects a moment, and then takes her handbag and quickly rummages through it. He pulls out her wallet, from which he takes some photos, letters, money, and the train tickets. He looks at the photos: one of the little Olivier, and one of Nadine. He looks at Nadine's photo for a long time, and as if suddenly inspired, puts it in his pocket.

OLIVIER grabs a sandwich and, while eating, silently reads the letters from Elizabeth's handbag.

INT. DUVALS' HOUSE. LIVING ROOM. NIGHT. 8 yrs.

NADINE—now an attractive girl of eighteen—waits at the living room window for her mother to arrive with Olivier. The car's lights illuminate the window. She draws back, rushes to the living room door leading to the hall, and hides behind it. Noise of opening doors, voices of ELIZABETH and OLIVIER . . . ELIZABETH switches on the light. NADINE, seized with panic, presses flat against the wall.

ELIZABETH: Well, here you are at home . . .

Her voice is falsely jovial. OLIVIER puts a rather small bag on the floor and looks around. Tense, ELIZABETH watches him.

ELIZABETH: Do you recognize it?

NADINE sees OLIVIER shake his head.

ELIZABETH: Nadine must be asleep already. . . . She didn't have the strength to wait up, poor thing. But she's made dinner . . .
OLIVIER: I'm not hungry.
ELIZABETH: Do you want to wash up? The bathroom is on the left . .

OLIVIER (*interrupting her*): I remember.

ELIZABETH tries to take him in her arms, but he steps back rapidly, even rudely. She gives up her attempt. OLIVIER turns his eyes away, and at that moment, catches a glimpse of NADINE. She puts a finger to her lips. The boy doesn't understand, and throws up a questioning look. NADINE leaves the room.

ELIZABETH (*o.s.*): Olivier! Come, I'll show you where the towels are!

OLIVIER picks up his bag, and proceeds in the direction of the voice.

INT. DUVALS' HOUSE. OLIVIER'S ROOM. MORNING.

OLIVIER has been awake for some time. He looks around the room, filled with toys and objects that belonged to the little Olivier. He sits at the desk, which is much too small for him, looks at little Olivier's picture, and compares it to his own face in the mirror.

He hears the vacuum cleaner, and a noise from Nadine's room. Standing at the door which separates the two rooms, he puts his eye against the keyhole and sees NADINE'S eye, peering through the other side. She leaps back, and ties a handkerchief around the knob, covering the keyhole. OLIVIER smiles. He hears Elizabeth's voice.

ELIZABETH (*o.s.*): Nadine!

INT. DUVALS' HOUSE. NADINE'S ROOM. DAY.

NADINE is looking at her reflection in the mirror. We can't recognize her at once, because the glass is broken. The noise of the vacuum cleaner comes nearer, and stops in the hall, in front of Nadine's door. The mother knocks at the girl's door, which is locked from the inside.

ELIZABETH: Nadine!
NADINE: Who are you calling, my little darling? Your daughter, or Olivier's sister? That makes two. Two Nadines who get mixed up.
ELIZABETH: Don't be foolish. Open up!
NADINE: The house is closed on Saturday.
ELIZABETH: Nadine!
NADINE: Well, all right.

NADINE finally opens the door and looks at ELIZABETH, who is holding the vacuum cleaner, still running. Her hair is pulled back, and she is wearing a clean apron.

NADINE: Well then? How is baby Jesus? Did you bring him back? Did you pamper him? Did you breast-feed him?

ELIZABETH is smiling somewhat foolishly; she wants to enter, but NADINE blocks her way. Her mother pushes her gently.

NADINE: I'll let you in, but leave your weapon outside.

ELIZABETH is so excited that NADINE can't spoil her mood. She sets down the vacuum cleaner, and goes in. She hugs NADINE tightly and looks around; the mess is indescribable. There is a snake in a box, a hamster in a cage, and an aquarium. NADINE sighs and, still wrapped in a sheet, curls up on the bed. Her mother begins to tidy up the room energetically. She puts some of Nadine's things on a shelf, others on the table, and throws some tights and a shirt to her daughter.

ELIZABETH: Put these on! . . . And this . . .

NADINE sighs as she catches it all and puts it by her side.

NADINE: What is this, a new regime?

ELIZABETH goes to the window, which she opens wide.

ELIZABETH: We can smell your menagerie . . . really, for a young girl's room . . .

NADINE springs up.

NADINE: Close that window!
ELIZABETH: What?
NADINE: Close it. I'm cold, do you understand? I can't stand drafts.
ELIZABETH: Stop! Get dressed . . .

NADINE interrupts her, runs to the window, and closes it; ELIZABETH struggles to reopen it; it's a close battle. NADINE ends up entirely naked, pulling her mother down and tickling her violently.

ELIZABETH: Nadine, stop please . . . have you gone crazy or what?
NADINE: Are you going to close the window? Answer: are you going to close it?

ELIZABETH begins laughing. NADINE, leaning over her, lifts her eyes and notices OLIVIER, standing in the half-open doorway and looking at the two women tangled up on the floor. NADINE gets up, reaches for the sheet, and covers herself up. ELIZABETH gets up too, and smoothes out her clothes with a nervous laugh. All three look at one another. At last ELIZABETH timidly breaks the embarrassed silence.

ELIZABETH: Well then. . . . Say good morning to one another. . . . Give each other a kiss.

NADINE obeys; she approaches the boy, and from behind her sheet, she kisses him coldly on the cheek. OLIVIER smiles at her, and returns a sincere kiss. She makes a face.

ELIZABETH: Nadine, go to Marcel and tell him to cut us a good Christmas tree, a big one. I'd like a wonderful Christmas.
NADINE: Don't you ever get tired of exploiting your slave?

ELIZABETH smiles at OLIVIER, as if to excuse her daughter.

ELIZABETH (*disapprovingly*): Nadine!
NADINE: I wasn't talking about me, I meant your "Man Friday."

She goes toward the door, picking up her things as she goes. ELIZABETH glances at OLIVIER, who has been watching them silently.

ELIZABETH: Maybe you could take your brother with you. He'd enjoy taking a tour . . .
OLIVIER: Yes . . . certainly . . .

EXT. IN FRONT OF THE DUVALS' HOUSE/FIELD/FOREST. DAY.

OLIVIER closes the gate to the fence surrounding the Duvals' house. NADINE crosses the road and disappears in the bushes on the other side. Marcel's house is behind the trees. OLIVIER wants to follow her, but he has to give way to three cars, one of which is a speeding police car. At the sight of police, OLIVIER withdraws instinctively, but immediately realizing his foolishness, he laughs to himself.

He runs across the road and reaches the trees, expecting to find Nadine, but there is no one there. He runs toward a hilly open space where two roads cross. He is wondering which one to take, when he sees Nadine's scarf lying on one of the roads. He smiles, picks it up, and follows the road, holding the scarf in his hand. He enters the woods, and suddenly hears the noise of breaking twigs behind him. Out of breath, he turns around, and changes direction.

OLIVIER: Nadine! Wait!

No answer. OLIVIER slows down. A BIRD flies up from under his feet. OLIVIER listens closely. He hears a faint noise coming from a ditch covered with dry grass. He smiles, kneels, crawls toward the edge of the ditch. He wants to surprise Nadine.

OLIVIER (*suddenly*): Whooaoo!

A large lump of earth thrown from below hits him on the forehead and breaks, dirtying his cheeks, getting into his mouth and eyes. Frightened, he pulls back. MARCEL, a shovel in his hand, appears in the ditch.

MARCEL: Hey! Who's crawling around here?

He sees OLIVIER, covered with mud, which he is trying to brush from his clothes. MARCEL smiles apologetically, showing his missing front tooth. He timidly helps OLIVIER to clean off the mud. Their eyes meet. MARCEL, embarrassed, lowers his eyes. He points to the scarf that OLIVIER is holding.

MARCEL: Wipe your face with that . . .
OLIVIER: It's not mine, it belongs to a girl. . . . Have you seen her?

MARCEL lifts his eyes and looks at him. Again he smiles his gap-toothed smile.

MARCEL: A girl? There aren't any girls around here.

MARCEL takes a crumpled pack of cigarettes out of his pocket and lights one. OLIVIER reaches for the pack.

OLIVIER: Do you mind?

And without waiting for an answer, he takes a cigarette, lights it on MARCEL's, and draws greedily. OLIVIER looks around.

OLIVIER: She must have passed by here . . . Nadine . . .

MARCEL casts a questioning glance at him.

OLIVIER: My sister.
MARCEL: Nadine?

MARCEL looks so bewildered that OLIVIER is amused.

OLIVIER: It's me, Olivier.

MARCEL is stunned.

MARCEL (*murmurs almost imperceptibly*): But Olivier's disappeared.
OLIVIER: Sorry, I've come back.

OLIVIER hears a noise of breaking twigs. He turns around and sees NADINE running away; she has been watching them from her hiding place. He throws his butt away and runs after her. He enters the forest. Out of breath, he looks around. Silence.

OLIVIER: Listen a minute, you! I'm not playing anymore.

Nobody answers. OLIVIER sits down on a tree trunk. He hears steps behind him. NADINE is coming from behind the bushes with a slow and calm step. Her hair is in disarray, and her eyes are red as if she's been crying. OLIVIER gets up and looks at her.

NADINE (*angrily*): Let's go home!

OLIVIER offers her the scarf.

OLIVIER: Here. It's yours . . .
NADINE: Keep it as a souvenir . . .

They walk for a while in silence.

OLIVIER: Don't we have to go to that . . . Marcel?

NADINE stops and looks at him.

OLIVIER: For the Christmas tree, or something?

NADINE, doubtful, looks at him closely. OLIVIER suddenly realizes that he has fallen into a trap.

OLIVIER: It was that guy? The one with the shovel?

NADINE doesn't answer.

OLIVIER (*trying to justify himself*): I didn't recognize him . . . You understand, after all these years.
NADINE: You couldn't recognize him. He came here after you left.
OLIVIER: Ah, you see . . .

The tension has eased. OLIVIER, in good spirits, walks beside Nadine, fidgeting with the scarf. Suddenly, NADINE grabs the scarf from him. OLIVIER looks at her, surprised.

NADINE: As a preventive measure. In case you hang yourself, it won't be my fault.

They walk in silence. A taxi that is going toward their house overtakes them. NADINE notices it, and without saying a word, or paying any attention to Olivier, runs after it. OLIVIER hesitates a moment, and runs after her. They reach the courtyard at the same time that SERGE, tan, balder, is taking his luggage from the taxi, helped by the DRIVER—two large suitcases and a trunk. He hears the pounding footsteps and turns around. His packages fall from his hands. NADINE has stopped a few steps from him, suddenly intimidated: SERGE does not look at her, he looks at the boy. Silence. SERGE moves a few steps toward him.

SERGE (*softly, with a lump in his throat*): Do you recognize me?

OLIVIER looks at him.

OLIVIER (*gravely*): Dad . . .

SERGE gives a deep, spasmodic sigh. He runs to embrace the boy tightly. NADINE watches them sulkily, with real pain in her expression. OLIVIER stands stiffly. He doesn't return the embrace. He looks at NADINE and suddenly winks at her knowingly over SERGE'S shoulder. She lowers her eyes.

INT. DUVALS' HOUSE. KITCHEN/LIVING ROOM. DAY.

Bright sun shines in the window. ELIZABETH is preparing the Christmas Eve dinner. SERGE is leaning against the kitchen sink. They speak softly, almost murmuring.

SERGE: And you didn't ask him anything?
ELIZABETH: No . . . do I ask *you* anything?
SERGE: But I have nothing to hide.
ELIZABETH: Really?
SERGE: We need to know why he did it and where he's been. . . . Why he didn't give us any sign that he was alive . . .
ELIZABETH: Serge, I'm afraid. He is so . . . so independent. I'm afraid that if we ask him questions, he'll run away again.
SERGE: But we have to . . . for our friends . . . for the neighbors. After all, we can't pretend . . . that nothing has happened. He has to

live here . . . go to school. . . . What do I know . . .
ELIZABETH: In any case, you'll be going 3,000 miles away. You won't have to . . . save face. That's my business.

SERGE lowers his head in silence. She feels sorry for him.

ELIZABETH: What if we all went away with you? Oh! Not for long . . . just for appearances.
SERGE: I'm not going back. Chad is finished for me. I feel like an even bigger nothing there than I am here.
ELIZABETH: That isn't true. You're not nothing.

SERGE squeezes her hand furtively.

SERGE: We could sell mother's house, and with that extra money, we could buy an apartment in Paris . . .

Music, at first hesitant, then louder and clearer, reaches them from the living room. It is OLIVIER, who is playing a tune on Elizabeth's old piano, first with one finger, then more and more proficiently. ELIZABETH stands at the kitchen door, her hands covered in dough. SERGE is behind her. She looks at him with a demented light in her eyes.

ELIZABETH (*murmurs*): How things change. . . . Do you remember, we thought that he didn't have an ear for music.
SERGE: He gets it from you. . . . He's talented at music, like his mother . . .

OLIVIER sees them. He quickly bangs the piano cover shut.

ELIZABETH (*in a falsely indifferent voice*): Have you seen Nadine?
OLIVIER: She's been in the bathroom . . . (*he looks at the clock*) for about two hours.
ELIZABETH: As usual. Nadine!

She goes to the bathroom and knocks on the door.

ELIZABETH: You're coming out of there, Nadine!

NADINE, in her bathrobe, comes out of the bathroom, passes by OLIVIER, and, without saying a word, turns on the TV.

Through the window, we see MARCEL coming across the fields with an enormous Christmas tree. ELIZABETH sees him and runs to open the door. He steps into the doorway, hiding timidly behind the tree. OLIVIER watches him attentively.

ELIZABETH: Come in . . . come in. . . . How beautiful it is! Serge! Marcel has brought us a tree.

SERGE takes the tree.

SERGE: Thank you, Marcel, for everything you've done for them.
ELIZABETH: Oh, Marcel, he's one of the family now. You'll come for Christmas Eve dinner, Marcel, as usual.
SERGE: Please don't hesitate.
MARCEL: No! I've already. . . . Goodbye!
ELIZABETH: Then we'll see you tomorrow, Marcel!

He casts a glance at Olivier, and runs out.

SERGE: Goodbye. Thank you!

SERGE leans the tree against the wall and turns to OLIVIER.

SERGE: Marcel was upset, the day you disappeared. He saw you last, do you remember?

OLIVIER doesn't answer. He looks at NADINE—she winks at him, letting him know that she had fooled him the previous day.

SERGE: Nadine, do we have a stand somewhere?

Before Nadine can answer, the doorbell rings. She jumps from the sofa, runs to the door, and opens it.

On the doorstep is BABETTE, in a mohair hat, with PAUL, her eight-year-old brother. Without hiding her curiosity, she throws a look at OLIVIER.

BABETTE (*coquettishly*): I hope I'm not disturbing you?

ELIZABETH looks nostalgically at little PAUL.

ELIZABETH: Of course not. . . . Let's see . . .

BABETTE: Mother sends you a cake! . . .
ELIZABETH: Thank you . . .

She kisses BABETTE and little PAUL, who clearly doesn't like this emotional display.

ELIZABETH: Say, Olivier . . . you could pack up your old clothes and toys. Paul could use them.
BABETTE: I don't know if . . .
ELIZABETH: Why not? Olivier, take the boxes from the hall! (*To Babette*) Serge will drive you back. Help him, Paul.

SERGE puts on his jacket, and goes out the front way. OLIVIER takes the boxes and goes upstairs. PAUL goes after him. BABETTE follows them with her eyes, then looks at NADINE, who, serious, almost gloomy, doesn't return the look.

NADINE (*to her mother*): It's time for your medication, Mrs. New Order.

ELIZABETH, docile, goes to the kitchen. The two girls are alone. BABETTE is full of curiosity.

BABETTE: Well then?

NADINE shrugs her shoulders.

BABETTE: Your brother is great! He's really cute!
NADINE: Isn't he! Don't you find him too handsome for this family?

BABETTE snickers.

BABETTE: I saw that cop who found him, on TV. He said that he was pulled from the deepest decadence. Like in Zola, how about that! Say, bring him along to the New Year's party!

INT. DUVALS' HOUSE. OLIVIER'S ROOM. DAY.

OLIVIER empties the shelves and wardrobes. Earnestly, PAUL helps him to pack. OLIVIER glances at him from time to time. He whistles.

PAUL (*overcoming his shyness*): Is it true that you were carried off by extraterrestrials?
OLIVIER: Of course. How do you know?
PAUL: Nadine told me . . . and you were on another planet? All that time?

A small ball on which a clown's face is painted falls from the empty shelf. It bounces several times in the light, and lands with the face turned up.

INT. DUVALS' HOUSE. LIVING ROOM. LATE EVENING.

A fire is burning in the fireplace, some presents are lying beneath the Christmas tree, which is decorated with strings of lights.

The whole family plus MARCEL, silent and flushed, is gathered around the tree.

ELIZABETH picks up the packages one by one and reads the names. OLIVIER, in this atmosphere of family bliss, is somewhat awkward. NADINE doesn't take her eyes off him.

ELIZABETH: Olivier . . .

She gives him a present, which the boy unwraps. There are two fashionable shirts.

ELIZABETH: Marcel . . .

MARCEL opens his: a shirt with big checks. ELIZABETH opens her package and finds perfume. She looks at NADINE.

NADINE (*laughing*): I've decided that Mrs. New Order should change her perfume. A respectable matron. The head of the Duval clan.

ELIZABETH gives her a kiss, while SERGE picks up another large, flat package that looks like a picture.

SERGE: Olivier . . . and another one for Olivier . . .

He gives him a small package, which OLIVIER opens first. There are keys in it. OLIVIER looks at SERGE questioningly.

SERGE (*pleased and satisfied*): Look out the window.

OLIVIER runs to the window, through which we see, by the light of a street lamp, a new motor bike. He cries out in wonder and astonishment.

OLIVIER: Is it for me? Really?

He runs to Serge, and kisses him spontaneously. SERGE can hardly conceal his emotions.

SERGE: Well, and now something for Nadine. Wait . . .

He disappears into his study, and returns with a large package draped with a cloth, which he removes with a magician's flourish; it is a cage containing a small MONKEY. He takes out the animal and directs him toward NADINE. She has gotten up, and biting her lips, she looks at her father gravely. The MONKEY frees himself, and runs to NADINE's arms. ELIZABETH is astonished.

ELIZABETH: You see, it recognized you immediately!

NADINE holds the animal for a moment, then she pushes him away with a sort of disgust. The animal jumps from one object to the other, and everyone looks at him with interest.

In the meantime, ELIZABETH gives SERGE her present: a large book on Africa. OLIVIER has opened the flat package, glanced at it, then quickly looked at NADINE and wrapped it up again. SERGE leafs through the book, while ELIZABETH brings a bowl of punch from the kitchen. She pours for everyone. OLIVIER drinks his glass in one gulp. SERGE looks at him.

SERGE (*suddenly*): Now that everybody has their presents, don't you think, Olivier, that we have the right to hear you a little?

ELIZABETH freezes with the punch ladle in her hand. She casts a pleading glance at Serge.

ELIZABETH: Serge! . . .

MARCEL (*alarmed*): Well, I'll leave you.

SERGE: Don't go, Marcel. We don't have any secrets from you.

ELIZABETH: Serge, I beg you, let it go. Not today.
SERGE: There's nothing to be afraid of, is there, pal?

OLIVIER, who all the while has kept his eyes low, looks at SERGE.

OLIVIER (*provocatively*): No!

He throws a challenging look at Nadine and draws his breath.

OLIVIER (*with a big smile*): Well, to start with, I was carried away. By E.T. . . .

ELIZABETH and SERGE look at him uncomprehendingly.

SERGE: E.T.? . . . .
OLIVIER: Ask Nadine. She knows about it. Some extraterrestrials on a flying saucer.

NADINE is embarrassed, as if caught red-handed.

NADINE: If I were you, I wouldn't insist, Dad. It's not the best way.
ELIZABETH: Stop it! It's Christmas, it was going so well. . . . I beg you!
NADINE (*paying no attention to Elizabeth*): As far as I'm concerned, I'd prefer to know. I've chosen the testing method. Do you want to unwrap the present I gave you, Olivier?

She goes up to Olivier and picks up the flat package. She opens it up. Everybody looks at it. It is a large board divided into several parts. In the first part, there is a large photo of the Grandmother, with the question, "Who is this?"

NADINE (*reads*): a) mother's mother? b) father's mother? c) Aunt Rosalie from Grenoble? Question two: your favorite cap was: a) green? b) red? c) yellow? Question three: you had an appendectomy: a) when you were two years old? b) two months before you disappeared? c) never? Question four: in school, your best friend's name was: a) Jacques? . . .

ELIZABETH finally shakes off her torpor.

ELIZABETH: You're much worse than I thought; you're despicable.

NADINE: I just want to get this cleared up. I'm not afraid of the truth!
ELIZABETH: Apologize, immediately.
NADINE: Let him pass the test first.

OLIVIER doesn't flinch. His gaze is fixed on the fire.

SERGE: Calm down! Certainly, if Olivier wants he can answer. . . . Tomorrow, or the day after. It's fine, Nadine, that you want to refresh his memory, to let everything out of him . . . but now is not the moment, I beg of you . . .

NADINE turns toward him vehemently.

NADINE: I've always been struck by your resemblance to someone in the Holy Bible, a certain Pontius Pilate.

She goes out, banging the door. Long, awkward pause. SERGE finally gets up to join his daughter.

Silence. There is only the MONKEY, jumping from one place to another. OLIVIER stoops down to add some wood to the fire. ELIZABETH approaches him, and places her hand on his shoulder. OLIVIER turns toward her, his face pink from the heat.

OLIVIER: Nadine can't stand me.
ELIZABETH: She's jealous. She's always been jealous of you.
OLIVIER: I was your favorite!

ELIZABETH doesn't answer. She laughs nervously. She takes the box with the two shirts for Olivier, and hands them to him, and the other box to Marcel.

ELIZABETH: Go on, men, try them on. I want to know if I chose well.

OLIVIER unbuttons his shirt and takes it off, facing ELIZABETH. MARCEL tries his on, turning his back.

OLIVIER: Tell me, what was I like when I was little?
ELIZABETH (*to Marcel*): He was very affectionate. . . . Very happy during the day, but at night he was afraid. He didn't want to sleep alone; that always made Serge upset.

OLIVIER listens while taking off his undershirt.

ELIZABETH: Of the two of you, Nadine was more of a boy.

OLIVIER has put on his new shirt while she was talking; he opens the fly of his jeans to tuck his shirt in. Abruptly ELIZABETH stops, her eyes fixed on a small scar on his lower abdomen. Her voice is choked with emotion.

ELIZABETH: What is this?
OLIVIER: This?

He touches the scar.

ELIZABETH: But it is. . . . Oh! Olivier!

She runs toward him and embraces him joyfully. SERGE, who is coming downstairs, bumps into his wife, who now is running upstairs four steps at a time, very excited. SERGE catches her by the arms and stops her.

SERGE: Leave her alone now . . . she's calmed down. . . . She'll get over it.

But ELIZABETH doesn't listen to him.

ELIZABETH: Serge! He has an appendectomy scar! Exactly the same!

EXT. OUTSIDE DUVALS' HOUSE. NIGHT.

All the lights are out. MARCEL is walking around among the trees and watching. We see the house from his point of view.

INT. DUVALS' HOUSE. NADINE'S ROOM. NIGHT.

In her bed, NADINE sobs silently. She beats the pillow with her fists in a powerless rage.

INT. DUVALS' HOUSE. KITCHEN/LIVING ROOM. NIGHT.

OLIVIER, in his pajamas, is drinking water from the kitchen tap. He goes to the living room, looks around, opens a drawer, and leafs through the papers there. Under a box, he finds some 500 franc bills. He counts them rapidly, takes one, and puts the rest back. He takes a few papers, goes closer to the fire, which is still glowing in the hearth, and by its light, reads Elizabeth's large writing, which seems to be the beginnings of letters: the date and "Serge, come back!", "Serge, listen, I can't stand it any longer, Nadine is growing too fast, that scares me. At night . . . ", "I see that last evening when I sang 'The Angels' to him. . . . You ask me if I drink. That's a stupid question!"

OLIVIER puts back the letters. He goes to the piano and opens the top. He plays softly, with one finger, the little Olivier's song, mentioned by Elizabeth in her letter that was never mailed.

INT. DUVALS' HOUSE. PARENTS' BEDROOM. NIGHT.

The outline of the image is blurred. Through the keyhole we see the silhouettes of ELIZABETH and SERGE, who are undressing for bed. She looks up. She freezes, as if she has heard something. Then she looks at SERGE.

He finishes undressing and throws his clothes on the floor. He doesn't take his eyes off his wife. ELIZABETH lies down on her side of the bed and reaches out toward the lamp. She wants to switch it off, but he prevents her: he lies down across the bed, pulls her toward him hard, caressing her passionately.

SERGE: My dear . . . Elizabeth . . . my dear . . .

She defends herself weakly.

ELIZABETH: Let me go . . . Serge. . . . No. . . . please . . . not now . . . not yet . . .
SERGE: Now . . . yes. . . . I want it . . .

He pulls her against him even more strongly, rests his head on her shoulder and sobs briefly.

SERGE: How I missed you! You can't imagine how much I missed you. My love . . . my love.

Their breathing quickens; she doesn't resist any longer. They make love violently, with the bedside lamp still on.

INT. DUVALS' HOUSE. HALLWAY. NIGHT.

NADINE, her face puffy from crying, comes out of her room. She stops. In the shadows of the corridor she sees OLIVIER, who is peering through the slightly open door of his parents' bedroom.

OLIVIER has heard her approach and turns toward her, smiles knowingly at her, and motions for her to come near. NADINE bends down toward the slim beam of light. She sees her father's back, covered with sweat, moving in front of the headboard, and her mother's legs in the air.

NADINE jumps. OLIVIER, facing her, laughs silently, truly amused by what he has seen. NADINE clenches her teeth; she looks at him with intense hatred. He becomes serious and is able to withstand her gaze.

OLIVIER: Got a problem?

NADINE takes a bound, and slaps his face with all her might. He grabs her by the wrist and holds her tightly.

NADINE: Let go.

He holds on. They struggle silently.

OLIVIER (*hisses*): Well? You're afraid, huh? For the little family? Mama-hen? Daddy-cakes? You know what I could do with you? You know where I could . . .
NADINE: Let go!

She frees herself violently and bumps against the stairs. The door to the parents' room opens; SERGE, in a dressing gown, his face crimson, appears on the threshold. ELIZABETH's head appears behind him.

SERGE: What's happening here?

NADINE is silent; she is breathing heavily. OLIVIER smiles at SERGE with a large and sincere smile.

OLIVIER: Nothing.

SERGE: I'm warning you, Nadine, stop provoking him. You have to understand that you're not alone any more with your mother. You're not the one that makes the rules here any more.

NADINE reddens, turns her back, and slams her bedroom door noisily.

INT. DUVALS' HOUSE. NADINE'S ROOM/OLIVIER'S ROOM. NIGHT.

In her room, NADINE pushes the wardrobe against the door to barricade it. She blocks the door to the hall with her desk. A knock on the window. It is OLIVIER, who has reached there from the ledge. He holds onto the parapet and pushes the window open.

OLIVIER: Yoo-hoo! It's me!

Enraged, she runs to the window and shuts it with all her strength, pinching his fingers. He screams and disappears. Panic-stricken over what she has done, she opens the window wide and leans out.

OLIVIER, who has managed to squat on the ledge, protests, laughing. He takes NADINE in his arms, while he is still on the ledge, and kisses her very hard on the lips.

Eventually he releases her, both of them panting. She jumps back and wipes her lips violently, scornfully, as if she wanted to wipe away the kiss. He looks at her. His face changes expression: an evil, vexed look appears on it.

OLIVIER: You're too much . . . really, you're overdoing it.

He turns around slowly and makes his way cautiously along the ledge, toward his room. NADINE is alone. She crosses her arms on her breasts.

INT. DUVALS' HOUSE. KITCHEN. MORNING.

ELIZABETH, calm and looking younger, is making coffee. There are fresh croissants on the table. NADINE enters quietly and sits down at the table without a word. She chews a croissant, deliberately letting a lot of crumbs fall. Her mother is annoyed by the mess she is making, but abstains from any comment.

OLIVIER, wearing an undershirt, enters the kitchen, still sleepy. The MONKEY is sitting on his shoulder. NADINE lowers her eyes. OLIVIER smiles at ELIZABETH. She pours him some coffee. He takes a croissant and eats it hungrily. ELIZABETH watches him.

ELIZABETH: Is it good?

OLIVIER nods his head.

ELIZABETH: I remembered that you used to like them. I heated them in the oven. The way you liked it . . .

She touches his hair timidly, then withdraws her hand. NADINE is silent, her gaze fixed on the table; she is obstinately crumbling a croissant. OLIVIER looks at her obliquely. He eats a second croissant with gusto.

ELIZABETH: Nadine, stop making crumbs!
NADINE (*suddenly, as if talking to herself*): One thing astonishes me about you, my dear . . .

ELIZABETH blushes deeply.

NADINE: Maybe you don't have a lot going for you, but I thought that you at least had dignity.

ELIZABETH is silent. OLIVIER stops eating. He looks back and forth between the two women.

NADINE: They dropped you like an old sock, both of them; true or false? They got out and left us alone, you and me. And now they turn up, as if nothing had happened, and you lick their boots, and the rest of them, too.
ELIZABETH: Nadine, I'm begging you . . .

NADINE continues, coldly disdainful, without paying attention to her mother.

NADINE: I can't possibly understand how you could stoop so low. . . .

Poor little dear, you're quite ridiculous.
ELIZABETH: Watch what you say!
NADINE (*with tears in her eyes*): But we were fine together, you were happy with me, you always said so!
ELIZABETH (*crying*): What did you expect me to say? It was a nightmare, all those years! If I didn't kill myself, it was only for you!
NADINE: Poor little bimbo! You have them now, your guys. You can jump as high as you want!

OLIVIER doesn't take his eyes from them. He is amused. ELIZABETH meets his gaze. She controls her anger with difficulty.

ELIZABETH (*with a forced calm*): If someday you're capable of loving someone besides yourself, you'll understand.
NADINE: Never!

NADINE gets up and leaves the room without another word, closing the door behind her.

ELIZABETH follows her with her eyes, then turns to the window. She sees her little OLIVIER, in his red cap, laughing as he swings. Startled, she turns toward OLIVIER, who has just finished his breakfast.

ELIZABETH (*matter-of-factly*): You know, Olivier, you should know this. This isn't blackmail, but . . . if you do it again. . . . If. . . . I won't be able to stand the blow.

EXT. ROAD THROUGH THE FIELDS. MORNING.

NADINE is walking with a confident gait, swinging her arms. She hears the noise of a motor. OLIVIER is coming toward her on his motorbike. When he is abreast of her, he slows up. She pretends not to see him.

OLIVIER: Will you get on? Dear?

She doesn't falter. He begins to make smaller and smaller circles around her, trying to make her laugh. But she continues to ignore him. In the distance, BABETTE and PAUL appear. OLIVIER glances at NADINE again, and accelerates rapidly. He brakes near BABETTE, who welcomes him with a big smile.

BABETTE: It's yours? Congratulations . . .
OLIVIER: Yeah. A bribe for the prodigal son, as Nadine says. Want to go for a ride?

BABETTE agrees immediately. She puts little PAUL on the motorbike, then seats herself behind him. She hugs his waist tightly. They start up. She laughs loudly. NADINE stops and watches them as they disappear. She turns back toward the house with a heavy step.

EXT. VILLAGE SQUARE. MORNING.

OLIVIER, little PAUL, who is enchanted by the expedition, and BABETTE arrive on the motorbike at the square. BABETTE gets down and helps the little boy off. OLIVIER looks around him. Faces in the café windows are watching him. He returns their gaze. Some MEN come out of the bar and also look at him, with open curiosity. OLIVIER smiles at them insolently, and raises his hand as if in greeting. He turns to the WOMEN behind the windows, and bows very low, as if taking a curtain call. BABETTE laughs, delighted by his arrogance.

EXT./INT. DUVALS' HOUSE. GARAGE. DAY.

OLIVIER approaches the house and takes his motorbike into the garage. He is lost in his thoughts. In the garage, SERGE is rummaging among piles of old inner tubes and tools. He notices OLIVIER.

SERGE: What a mess! As soon as your back is turned. . . . Will you help me clean it up, Olivier?

OLIVIER pretends not to have heard. SERGE clears a path for himself through the mess, so that he can reach the corner. At last, he pulls out a bottle of Calvados. It's dusty; the label is partly torn off.

SERGE (*triumphantly*): Look at that! It was there! All that time! I remembered that it must be here, somewhere. . . . Look.

OLIVIER comes nearer.

SERGE: I didn't want to keep alcohol in the house. Because of Mom, you know? Don't say anything to her, of course. It'll be our secret.

OLIVIER smiles in spite of himself—Serge's behavior is so naive. SERGE tries with all his strength to remove the cork, but doesn't succeed. OLIVIER takes the bottle from him, places it between his thighs, squeezes, removes the cork with one movement, and gives the bottle to SERGE.

SERGE: You're strong, huh?
OLIVIER: I have strong arms. I always did, when I was little . . .

He is silent, suddenly embarrassed. SERGE has noticed nothing. He drinks from the bottle. Delighted, he blinks his eyes.

SERGE: Terrific! Do you want some?

They sit down on the tires and drink, passing the bottle back and forth.

SERGE: Just what I needed. It's my uncle's Calvados, Uncle Jean from Normandy, do you remember him?

OLIVIER looks at SERGE with focused attention.

OLIVIER (*demanding*): Why did you leave? When . . . I ran away?

SERGE doesn't answer.

OLIVIER: It wasn't nice . . . going away at a time like that. You cleared out, didn't you? Like a coward.

He takes the bottle from SERGE and drinks in huge gulps.

SERGE: You ran away too.
OLIVIER (*laughing ironically*): Me, that's different. I was young.
SERGE: I thought that a trip like that could change things.
OLIVIER: Is it different in Africa?
SERGE: It's even worse. But that's something I only realize now. Basically, it wasn't worth the trouble. It's better to stay in your own place, and keep yourself in control. (*He grabs Olivier's hand*) You like to travel, don't you?

OLIVIER: I especially love train stations. I used to love them, anyway.
SERGE: And now?
OLIVIER: I don't really know.
SERGE: You want the world to be different, I suppose?
OLIVIER: Stupid idea! I don't give a damn.
SERGE: You know, people think that women are weak. But they're really tough! My mother, for example. Your grandmother. Before I left for Africa, I put her in a retirement home. I thought that would be on my conscience for the rest of my life, that she would die within a month. And what do you know? She lived another five years—she died just last year. And furthermore, she dredged up a little old guy, they got married, and she left everything to him, except her house. Pretty amazing!

Both of them burst out laughing. OLIVIER takes out a pack of cigarettes and offers them to SERGE. They smoke together.

OLIVIER: Why did she get remarried? At her age!
SERGE: You know, people are afraid of loneliness. . . . Especially women. They need somebody, so they can crush him.
OLIVIER: And Mom?
SERGE: What about Mom?
OLIVIER: She was alone when you left her.
SERGE: There was . . . Nadine.
OLIVIER (*laughing*): Not easy to crush that one!

Through the open door, we see ELIZABETH coming out and getting in the car. SERGE pulls OLIVIER along like a fellow-conspirator, and they hide behind a pile of tires.

SERGE: Be careful, she might see us . . .

Noise of the car starting up and driving off.

INT. DUVALS' HOUSE. OLIVIER'S ROOM. DAY.

NADINE has pulled Olivier's bag out from under the bed and is rummaging in it. It is almost empty: some dirty socks, a subway map, a 500 franc bill, some business cards, and at the bottom, she finds her own photograph, wrapped in some paper. She looks at it, bewildered. She hears a door creak downstairs, and her mother's voice.

ELIZABETH (*o.s.*): Olivier! Serge! Nadine!

INT. DUVALS' HOUSE. LIVING ROOM. EVENING.

*A fire is burning in the hearth; there is an opera on TV—*Boris Godunov. *ELIZABETH is looking out the window trying to make out something in the dark. Then she turns toward NADINE, who is lying on the sofa in front of the TV.*

ELIZABETH: They didn't say where they were going?
NADINE: You really can't do without them, can you?
ELIZABETH: Did they leave on the motorbike?

NADINE shrugs. She gets up, goes toward the fireplace, and stretches her arms out toward the fire.

ELIZABETH: Say, Nadine. . . . Could something have happened to them? Maybe we should call the police?

NADINE goes toward the door and opens it, then she turns toward her mother.

NADINE: I know one thing. If I was as afraid of life as you are, I'd shoot myself!

ELIZABETH presses the remote control hard, and the opera is gone. In the sudden silence, we hear singing. ELIZABETH freezes for a moment, then moves quickly. She and NADINE rush toward the door.

INT. DUVALS' HOUSE. GARAGE. EVENING.

ELIZABETH and NADINE enter the garage. OLIVIER and SERGE, completely drunk, are bellowing an English song together. SERGE notices his wife.

SERGE (*with an apologetic smile*): Elizabeth. . . . We're a little bit. . . .

Olivier! Sing for your mother . . . he has a very good accent, you know!

He tries to get up to take ELIZABETH in his arms, but stumbles and falls at her feet. OLIVIER is laughing drunkenly.

OLIVIER (*singing*): "My mother was a tailor, she sew my new blue jeans . . . My father was a gambling man, down in New Orleans . . ."

INT. DUVALS' HOUSE. PARENTS' ROOM. NIGHT.

In the bedroom, ELIZABETH is holding SERGE'S head, while he leans over the edge of the bed and vomits into a basin. NADINE hands her a damp towel, which she puts on the nape of her husband's neck.

ELIZABETH (*emphatically*): You see. . . . You know very well it's no good for you. You know that you can't take it . . .

SERGE moans and falls back on the bed. NADINE takes the towel, and leaves.

INT. DUVALS' HOUSE. BATHROOM/CORRIDOR. NIGHT.

NADINE holds the towel under cold water. As she is returning, she sees OLIVIER, holding the MONKEY, standing in the doorway, blocking her passage. She tries to go by him, but he laughs and blocks her way.

NADINE: Let me through.
OLIVIER: We have to talk. I want to know . . .

He releases the MONKEY, who jumps onto the sink. OLIVIER looks NADINE straight in the eyes.

NADINE: Go to bed. You're drunk.
OLIVIER: Why don't you like me?
NADINE: You've won over Mom, Dad, Babette, little Paul, even the monkey. But I don't have to love you.

OLIVIER comes nearer to her. They look at one another.

OLIVIER: You think I'm not your brother?
NADINE: No.

OLIVIER: You've never been able to stand me. You really wanted me to disappear.

NADINE blushes deeply.

NADINE: That's not true! . . . Olivier was different. You're not like him.
OLIVIER: Why would I pretend to be your brother?
NADINE (*slowly, thoughtfully*): I don't know.

He smiles. He reaches toward her. She recoils. He tries to come closer, bringing his hand near her face. He wants to touch her, but can't, as if her look were stopping his hand. NADINE stares at him with a bizarre expression.

OLIVIER: What's happening to you?

He struggles hard to approach her, but still an invisible force prevents him. He lowers his arm.

OLIVIER (*astonished*): How . . . do you manage to do that?
ELIZABETH (*o.s.*): Nadine! The towel!

NADINE appears ready to faint. She leans heavily on the bathtub. She throws the wet towel to Olivier.

NADINE: Go bring it to her.

OLIVIER goes out obediently. NADINE sits limply on the tub. She hides her face in her hands. The MONKEY watches her with his grave, unmoving eyes.

INT. DUVALS' HOUSE. NADINE'S/OLIVIER'S ROOMS. NIGHT.

NADINE is sitting up in bed, unable to fall asleep. She hears sobbing coming from Olivier's room. She gets up, and knocks on the door.

NADINE: Are you asleep?

No response. Only louder sobbing. She turns the door handle, goes into Olivier's room, and turns on the overhead light.

OLIVIER, racked by spasmodic sobs, is curled up on the bed, which is short for him. His head is under the pillow. NADINE, alarmed, leans over him.

NADINE: What's the matter with you? Do you want me to call Mom?

He doesn't answer. He curls up tighter.
A still louder sob. She, not knowing what to do, passes her hand over Olivier's hair, which is damp with sweat. His hand comes out from under the comforter. She takes his hand in hers, and sits on the edge of the bed. He rolls into a ball, and puts his head in her lap. She shudders.

NADINE: Come on, stop it.

She caresses his head. He stops crying. She is very still.

NADINE (*demanding*): Are you really crying, or only pretending?

He raises his head and leans on his elbow. He suddenly looks at her and smiles. His face is wet with tears.

OLIVIER: When I drink, it always makes me cry.
NADINE: Why?
OLIVIER: I don't know . . .

He suddenly leans over and pulls Nadine's Christmas present—the board with questions—out from under the bed. He lays it on his lap.

OLIVIER: That's Mamie, Dad's mother. My cap was red. I had my appendix out two months before I disappeared. My friend was Jacques.
NADINE: That doesn't mean anything now. You've had a lot of time to find out.

He throws the board down, and suddenly starts to laugh. She looks at him, frowning. Finally, she bursts out laughing too.

OLIVIER: Why are you laughing?
NADINE: Why are you?
OLIVIER: At you!
NADINE: No, at you! You're dumb.

She gets up. He grabs her arm.

OLIVIER: Stay a little longer . . .
NADINE: If you'll tell me what happened. What did you do in Paris? I want to know more about homos.
OLIVIER: And you're going to tell me how you did it . . . so that I couldn't touch you.

She thinks a moment.

NADINE: Look.

She raises her head, and fixes her eyes on the ceiling light, which is on. She directs her half-closed eyes at the bulb. Beads of sweat stand out on her face. OLIVIER follows her gaze. Suddenly, the bulb moves, and slowly, very slowly, it turns. NADINE holds her breath; the bulb comes unscrewed and falls to the floor with a loud crash. In the darkness, OLIVIER'S enthusiastic cry is heard. He turns on his bedside lamp and looks around at the empty room. Nadine is gone.

OLIVIER: Nadine!

NADINE, in her bed, laughs, her head buried in the pillow. The door to Olivier's room opens, and OLIVIER stands in the light. He comes toward her bed, sits down on it, and quickly slides under the comforter. She sits up quickly.

NADINE: Have you gone crazy? What are you doing?
OLIVIER: I'm afraid, all alone. Warm me up a little. Come on, move over.

She is silent. She has a strange, dreamy smile. He lies on top of her and embraces her tightly. They stay like that a while. She doesn't move; she holds her breath.

OLIVIER: You smell nice.

NADINE doesn't answer. She closes her eyes.

OLIVIER: Have you been able to do that for a long time? I mean, with the lamp?
NADINE: After you left . . . I was often very angry. . . . I would stamp my feet, bang my head against the walls. And one day, I noticed that

instead of doing all that, I could make things move from far away, and I didn't need to have fits anymore. After that, everything was fine . . . with Mom. And now, she says that all that time she only wanted to shoot herself. She betrayed me, do you understand?

OLIVIER: Those are only words . . . shoot yourself. . . . I've said it, too.

He stops.

NADINE: No, she would have been capable . . .

Suddenly, she moves. She laughs softly.

OLIVIER: What's the matter?

NADINE: I can feel. . . . I think we're not the right age anymore, to sleep in the same bed.

OLIVIER sits up suddenly in the bed. He is very embarrassed. NADINE turns toward him and looks at him closely.

NADINE: You're not a child anymore. I'm not, either. And then, you're my brother.

He starts to get up out of the bed.

She takes him gently by the shoulder.

NADINE: You don't have to go, just turn the other way.

He obediently turns his back to her. She cuddles against him. They lie there in silence. Her eyes are wide open. She reaches out and gently caresses him. He turns around quickly, pulls her toward him, and gives her a long kiss.

OLIVIER: Now you know how homos kiss.

She closes her eyes. She offers no resistance.

INT. DUVALS' HOUSE. NADINE'S ROOM. DAWN.

Olivier's hand moves very slowly on Nadine's naked body. He caresses the mark on her breast: the scar from the cigarette burn on the night of her brother's disappearance.

OLIVIER: What's that?
NADINE (*whispers*): A sacrifice.

He kisses the scar.

NADINE: I didn't think it would be that good with a man.
OLIVIER: I'm not a man. I'm a boy.

INT./EXT. DUVALS' HOUSE. SERGE'S OFFICE/FRONT YARD. DAY.

NADINE is standing at the window. She is looking out at the yard, where OLIVIER is playing with little PAUL, enjoying himself as much as the little boy. Mechanically, NADINE writes on the glass: I.L.Y. She sees OLIVIER and PAUL peeing together.

OLIVIER: Do you know what I do when I'm sick of someone? I pee at him, like this (*pees and sings*): "Pee-pee on the grass, to bug the ladybugs. Pee-pee on the grass, to bug the butterflies . . ."

NADINE turns away from the window as SERGE enters, still pale after his drinking bout the evening before, shame-faced and sleepy.

SERGE: Do you know what time it is?
NADINE: It's already four.
SERGE: I didn't wake up.

She pays no attention to what he is saying.

NADINE: Do you remember Olivier's peeing contests?
SERGE: Peeing?
NADINE: Yes, long-distance peeing! He was very proud of it! Marcel taught him, remember? They had contests with Jacques.
SERGE: Really? I don't remember. . . . Peeing?

She leans on the window sill.

NADINE (*very low*): It's him. It's Olivier.

There is an expression of happiness on her father's face.

SERGE: See? You didn't want to believe it. . . . My little girl.

Over her shoulder, he reads the letters she has written on the glass.

SERGE: Let me guess. I.L.Y—I love you. Am I right? I love you too . . . very much.

He hugs her, moved. She disengages herself. She is almost crying in her despair.

NADINE: You never understand anything!

NADINE runs out of the room. SERGE wears a look of comic disbelief. He turns to the MONKEY, who is eating a banana.

SERGE: Ah! Women . . .

EXT./INT. ROAD BY MARCEL'S HOUSE/MARCEL'S KITCHEN. EVENING.

OLIVIER, on the motorbike, is returning from the village. He slows down near Marcel's house, where he sees a light. He stops the motorbike, dismounts from it, approaches the door, and knocks.

OLIVIER: Marcel! Are you there?

No answer. He knocks again.

OLIVIER: Marcel! It's me, Olivier! Do you have any cigarettes? The tobacco shop is already closed.

Suddenly he hears the desperate cry of a child, coming from the house. OLIVIER presses his eye to the door. The cry comes again, this time muffled. He throws himself against the door as hard as he can. The bolt gives way, and OLIVIER bursts into Marcel's kitchen.

At a glance, he sees MARCEL, who, with a strange and distant expression on his face, is holding down little PAUL on the dirty tiles of the kitchen floor. One of MARCEL'S hands is plastered over the child's face. As he catches sight of OLIVIER, PAUL gives a desperate moan.

MARCEL notices OLIVIER only at that moment. He gets up and tries to run away, tripping over his lowered pants. PAUL crawls toward

OLIVIER, who grabs a shovel from the corner, and in a bound, is next to MARCEL. OLIVIER hits him with all his strength with the shovel. MARCEL is knocked unconscious. OLIVIER returns to PAUL and takes him in his arms.

OLIVIER: It's over. Everything's okay. He won't do anything more to you.
PAUL (*sobs*): I was going back home when he called me—he said . . . that he had something for me . . . and after . . . after . . .

OLIVIER's expression changes; he has just understood something. He looks at the unconscious MARCEL. He gets up, picks up a rope lying in a corner. He stuffs a dishcloth in Marcel's mouth, ties him up, and turns toward PAUL.

OLIVIER: We'll leave him here and go to Paris. Okay?

Paul's face lights up.

PAUL: Right now? You and me? On the bike?

EXT. POLICE STATION IN PARIS. NIGHT.

Little PAUL, in Olivier's jacket, which is too big for him, is waiting in the street in front of the police station. He is watching the motorbike.

Through the glass door, he sees OLIVIER, who is arguing with the POLICEMAN on duty. The POLICEMAN shrugs his shoulders, finally picks up the telephone, says something, and hands the receiver to OLIVIER. OLIVIER explains something, then hands the receiver to the POLICEMAN, who assents, and writes something on a piece of paper that he gives to OLIVIER. He takes the paper, and runs out. He helps PAUL onto the motorbike, and starts the motor.

PAUL: Where are we going now?
OLIVIER: To a cop's house . . . he'll give you something to eat . . . you'll see . . .
PAUL: I want to go back . . .

OLIVIER doesn't answer. He starts off. PAUL hangs onto him tightly.

INT. DRUOT'S APARTMENT. NIGHT.

DRUOT, in his pajamas, opens the door of his apartment to OLIVIER, who is dirty and covered with dust. He propels PAUL in front of him. DRUOT casts an alarmed glance at the little boy.

DRUOT: What happened, anyway?
OLIVIER: Do you have a bathroom here? He has to go pee-pee.
DRUOT: It's over there.

He points. OLIVIER helps PAUL to take off his jacket, then he nudges him toward the bathroom.

OLIVIER: Go . . . you know how to get your pants down, I guess?

PAUL is amused by the silly joke. He goes obediently into the bathroom. He closes the door behind him.

OLIVIER: Do you remember Marcel? He was the last one . . .
DRUOT: I remember.
OLIVIER: He was after the little guy. He's a pervert. I happened by there . . . at the last moment. And the . . . I came because . . . (*he hesitates a moment, then declares firmly*) I think he did the same thing to little Olivier.

DRUOT looks at him, bewildered.

DRUOT: What do you mean, to little Olivier?

OLIVIER raises his voice. He is desperate.

OLIVIER: You don't understand? It isn't me! I'm not the real one! I was only pretending!

INT. DRUOT'S APARTMENT. DAWN.

PAUL, covered by a blanket, is sleeping on Druot's bed. Druot's bedroom is not very big, not very clean, shabby. Some objects, books, and papers are lying on the floor. OLIVIER is seated next to a low table, facing the inspector who, pale, wrapped tightly in his bathrobe, doesn't take his eyes from OLIVIER, who slowly drinks a bottle of beer. He is avoiding DRUOT's gaze.

OLIVIER: I thought that cops . . .

He stops. DRUOT smiles sadly. He finishes the thought for Olivier.

DRUOT: . . . live better, huh? I'm not a very successful cop. You were supposed to be my biggest success.

OLIVIER finishes the beer, and wipes off the wet mark left by the bottle.

DRUOT: Do you want another?
OLIVIER: What should I do now?
DRUOT: What can you do? I'll call police headquarters. . . . We have to phone the Duvals . . . and the kid's parents. They must be sick with worry.
OLIVIER: I thought . . .
DRUOT: You thought what?
OLIVIER: That maybe we could hide it . . . so they wouldn't find out. She could never stand it!
DRUOT: What do you mean, she?
OLIVIER: Mom—Madame Duval.

DRUOT shrugs his shoulders.

DRUOT: How could you hide it? And what for? You'd keep on pretending to be their son?
OLIVIER: Oh, I know . . . it's not possible . . . but I thought . . .

He is silent, and breathing heavily. PAUL turns in the bed, and moans in his sleep. OLIVIER looks at him, and goes to him to adjust the blanket.

DRUOT: Why did you do it?
OLIVIER: Do what?
DRUOT: Why did you pretend?
OLIVIER (*interrupting*): Why? Why? To make you happy! It was what you wanted, right? It suited everybody! Then, for a while, I was a nice little boy. Then it got real.

INT. MARCEL'S HOUSE. DAY.

The room is full of POLICEMEN. SERGE and NADINE are also there.

MARCEL, very pale, seems diminished by his bandaged head. He is the first to descend the narrow stairs to the cellar. Two POLICEMEN with shovels follow him, then come inspector DRUOT, NADINE and SERGE together. NADINE and SERGE stop at the top of the stairs. They are trembling.

MARCEL pushes aside a box of potatoes and looks right and left—he hesitates. Silence. MARCEL indicates a spot where the earth is beaten down.

MARCEL: It's . . . there . . .

The two POLICEMEN start to dig. MARCEL directs entreating looks at the inspector. He tries hard to avoid meeting SERGE'S gaze.

MARCEL: I swear to you . . . I only wanted to touch him . . . and . . . he was afraid . . . he wanted to run away . . . run away . . . he fell down the stairs . . . he didn't see that the door was open . . . he didn't move at all. . . . I . . . I had to do something. . . . Afterwards I took his bike and his cap . . . I didn't bury them . . . I left them in the woods . . . I didn't know what to do . . . I wanted to forget. . . . It wasn't my fault! Me . . . I loved the kid a lot! And she . . . Elizabeth . . . I . . .

MARCEL is shaken with sobs, choking on his words.

MARCEL: And now . . . when he came back. . . . It's . . . as if . . . I was going crazy . . . as if someone. . . . It's not my fault!

The POLICEMEN find something. They draw back, and look at the inspector. From above, NADINE catches sight of the little white skeleton in the hole. SERGE takes a step closer to the excavation. He looks, then recoils abruptly, and faints, falling to the ground. NADINE attempts to catch him and is bending over him, along with DRUOT. She spits in the inspector's face.

EXT. IN FRONT OF MARCEL'S HOUSE. DAY.

A menacing crowd of FARMERS has assembled in front of Marcel's house. They look with sinister eyes at the POLICEMEN leading MAR-

CEL, who is handcuffed. He hides his face. Cries of hate, movement in the crowd.

OLIVIER and DRUOT are standing behind the people, a little to the side. They are watching MARCEL. OLIVIER sees SERGE come out of the house, wan, held up by NADINE. Instinctively, OLIVIER hides behind the crowd. He clenches his teeth. DRUOT watches him obliquely.

BABETTE and her PARENTS approach NADINE. The FARMERS surround them. BABETTE sees OLIVIER, and rushes angrily toward him.

BABETTE: Dirty cheat! Go away!

OLIVIER leaves. He starts to run across the fields. DRUOT follows him.

INT. HOTEL ROOM. EVENING.

Rain drums on the windowpanes. DRUOT and OLIVIER are in a small hotel room. Silently, they watch the news program about little Olivier's burial.

NEWSMAN: But the hope that the little boy had been found alive has proved vain. After six years, the body of the real Olivier Duval has been disinterred. The next-door neighbor has been confirmed to be the murderer.

On the screen, we see the country cemetery, ELIZABETH, supported by SERGE, the NEIGHBORS, NADINE. BABETTE, in tears, and PAUL are at her side. NADINE is hugging the MONKEY in her arms. Someone draws her aside.

OLIVIER: Nadine.

The news program moves to another story. DRUOT gets up quickly to turn off the set. The only sounds are rain against the window, and noisy shouts from the café below. DRUOT goes toward the window. He keeps on rubbing his forehead.

DRUOT: It's my fault . . . I let myself get carried away. I should have checked everything . . . the fingerprints . . . the dental records . . . done things by the book. . . . Simard was right. I'm not cut out for this job...

OLIVIER is silent.

DRUOT: You, in any case, have behaved very well. You should get the Legion of Honor.

OLIVIER doesn't respond. He gets up, and walks toward the door, taking his jacket. DRUOT's gaze follows him.

OLIVIER: I'm going now . . .

He puts his hand on the door handle.

DRUOT: Where?
OLIVIER: Home.

INT. DUVALS' HOUSE. KITCHEN. EVENING.

ELIZABETH is seated, with her hands resting on the table like a well-behaved schoolgirl. SERGE is near the stove, on which water is boiling. He hasn't taken off his hat; his eyes are red from crying.

NADINE enters the kitchen. The MONKEY is jumping around behind her. She avoids her parents' gaze, goes toward the stove, and turns off the gas under the pot of water. SERGE turns toward her with a strange grin on his face.

SERGE: You have it, your truth. Is it what you wanted?

NADINE doesn't answer. ELIZABETH is immobile, her gaze fixed on the dark window, beyond which a heavy rain falls. Silence. There is only the sound of rain on the glass.

The door opens noiselessly before OLIVIER. He is wet, muddy up to his knees. NADINE, then SERGE, see him. OLIVIER smiles at them. NADINE gives out a muffled cry. OLIVIER goes toward the table; he sits opposite ELIZABETH, and leans gently toward her. With a gesture that had belonged to little Olivier, he passes his palm in front of her eyes. ELIZABETH raises a questioning glance toward him. OLIVIER smiles at her, not without timidity.

OLIVIER: Come back to earth, Mom. I'm here.

ELIZABETH, once again fully present, says sweetly:

ELIZABETH: You're here, Olivier. You've come back after all.

Through the window we see little Olivier's empty swing. It is swinging, back and forth, against the darkness and rain.

THE END.

About the Script

In the beginning of *Olivier, Olivier* two children, Nadine and Olivier Duval—the sister age 9, the brother 8—are playing in a field. In their imaginary war with imaginary little green men, they pretend that a June bug is the enemy's transmitter, and Nadine crushes it with a stone. Olivier, in tears, watches the insect dying. Their neighbor, Marcel, rides past them on his bicycle, but now, in their game, he is an enemy spy. "He has the death ray," says Nadine. She aims a plastic tube at Marcel, making the sound of an explosion. "As if struck by Nadine's gaze, Marcel loses his balance and falls in a mud puddle." The children are delighted.

This is the *exposition*. It sets up the tone for the entire film: the interweaving of life and play, reality and fantasy—in *Olivier, Olivier* is dangerously interchangeable. The neighbor Marcel, indeed, "has the death ray." In less than twenty-four hours little Olivier will become his victim, as the June bug had been Nadine's.

The exposition also introduces the *place* where the action develops: the tranquil French countryside, with its forests and fields, and the *two main characters*: Nadine and Olivier. We realize right away that she is strong and determined: she crawls ahead of her brother, leading the way; she kills the June bug; she is, in fact, everything that the charmingly delicate and mischievous Olivier is not. She remains the same, strong and determined, when we see her six years later. And Olivier? Someone claiming to be Olivier comes to the Duvals. We are uncertain of who he is, and constantly switch between believing that he is Olivier and doubting it. We are alert and suspicious, like Nadine. But at a certain point, she gives up. And so do we.

In the screenplay there is a scene when Druot reads a description of Olivier's case to his superior, and the teenage boy in the cell can hear this. The scene has been cut from the film, which makes the boy's knowledge about the Duvals and about little Olivier's past more intriguing and ambiguous. Still, we, the viewers, know more than the family does. We see how habitually (or, should we say, professionally?) the boy rifles through Elizabeth's handbag while she is asleep on the train; and a few days later, in the Duvals' house, how adroitly he rummages through the drawer full of letters, stealing some of the money he finds there. Yet, we are inclined to believe that this young male prostitute and hustler is that same sweet little mama's boy, Olivier, who has just grown up and changed.

But *Olivier, Olivier* is not a suspense story. Rather, our guesses about Olivier's identity are inquiries into human nature: we wonder about the power of people's imagination over reality (Druot, and certainly Elizabeth and Serge, see in the teenager what they imagine is there). We contemplate the amazing transformations that people go through: This is how little Olivier turned out, we think. But then again, if this is an impostor, what was he like as a child? At what point did this second Olivier want to call Elizabeth "mom"? Did he know his own mother? Did he ever have a home? We ask ourselves these questions, consciously or unconsciously, while watching the film and after it is over. *Olivier, Olivier* is one of those films that will stay with you.

The story of the film can be summarized as follows:

One day a nice little boy, Olivier Duval, is sent to deliver lunch to his grandmother (like Little Red Riding Hood, he wears a red cap and carries a basket with food), and he disappears. This brings about the destruction of his family and causes great suffering to his mother. Six years later, police inspector Druot, who had unsuccessfully investigated the case, meets a teenaged street kid, a semi-criminal, whom he takes for Olivier. Neither Olivier's mother nor his father have any doubt that this is their son. Even the most perceptive member of the family, Olivier's sister Nadine, finally begins to believe it and even falls in love with the new Olivier. Accidentally, the boy figures out what must have happened to little Olivier; he reports it to the police and leaves the Duvals. Now the parents know that their little son was raped and murdered by their neighbor, Marcel, and that the second Olivier is an impostor. Nevertheless, when he returns, they accept him. They don't want to part with their illusion. "You are here, Olivier," says Elizabeth. "You've come back after all."

Now, this is a serious psychological game, while in reality "little Olivier's empty swing [is] swinging back and forth, against the darkness and rain."

There are infinite ways that a story can be shaped and structured into a screenplay. This is the function of the plot.

The plot of *Olivier, Olivier* is straightforward, without flashbacks or subplots. It looks deceptively simple. The flow of the action hides the underlying structural order.

The plot consists of the traditional *set-up, development,* and *resolution.*

It has an easily identifiable *catalyst*—Olivier's disappearance—the push that sets the action in motion. The plot also has two *turning points*: the first, when Druot "finds" Olivier, and the second, when Olivier reveals his true identity—which change the direction of the action and raise the screenplay's main dramatic question: "What happened to Olivier?" The climax answers that question—we see the little skeleton that was buried in Marcel's cellar.

The very specific element of the film's structure is its pattern of symmetry:

Two Oliviers;

Olivier, Olivier in the title;

Two games, which "frame" the plot—the children's game in the beginning and the adults' psychological game at the end;

Two time periods—the first when Olivier disappears, and the second six years later.

Note how the recurring motifs in the two time periods balance each other:

The first time period:	**The second time period:**
In the parents' bedroom, their irritation, almost animosity toward each other: "You are getting bizarre," says Serge, facing away from Elizabeth in bed. "You scare me."	The same bedroom, but now there is intimacy, love, even passion. "How I missed you!" Serge says. He doesn't take his eyes off his wife. "My love! My love!"
Nadine comforts little Olivier and takes him into her bed, when he has been "expelled from the Garden" of his mother's bed.	Nadine comforts the new Olivier when he cries ("When I drink, it always makes me cry," he says), and again she is in bed with him, but now in a very different way: they make love.
Marcel says that he was "completely out of smokes, so I called [Olivier] to bring me two packs."	The second Olivier knocks at Marcel's door and asks him if he has any cigarettes, saying, "The tobacco shop is already closed."
In the field, Nadine runs away and little Olivier, unable to keep up with her, shouts, "Nadine! Wait!"	In the same field, on the same road, Olivier shouts the same words to Nadine, trying to catch her.
Little Olivier is Marcel's victim.	Marcel's victim is little Paul, whom the second Olivier rescues at the last minute, thus, in a way, repaying his debt to his namesake.

From Elizabeth's story about Olivier's premature birth we learn that Serge fainted from joy when he learned that his son would live.

Serge faints from shock when he sees little Olivier's remains, which had been buried in Marcel's cellar.

Nadine, sitting at a cafe table with her father, writes the puzzling abbreviation I.H.Y.B. in melted ice cream, and Serge figures out that this stands for "I hate you, bastard."

Nadine writes on the window pane of Serge's office the abbreviation I.L.Y., which he immediately figures out to stand for "I love you," though he erroneously assumes that it is meant for him.

All these shifts in similar situations show with immediate clarity the changes that have taken place in the characters' relationships and actions. This makes the plot vigorous and unified.

In the film, there are four main characters: Nadine, Olivier, Elizabeth, and Serge; four secondary characters: Marcel, the neighbor, Druot, the police inspector, Babette, Nadine's friend, and Babette's younger brother, the eight-year-old Paul. There are also a few episodic characters.

In the screenplay there are more secondary and episodic characters, which were later excluded from the film. One of them is Nadine and Olivier's grandmother, a cranky and disagreeable old lady. There are three scenes with her in the screenplay.

The first one is near the beginning, when Serge, her son, visits her to give her dog an injection. Like any secondary character, she is important not for her own sake, but only in terms of her contribution to the whole story. The fact that she despises President Mitterand and the Socialists, that she doesn't like Elizabeth's cooking, that her sick, old dog Mimi is the only creature she cares about is irrelevant to the story. (Besides, giving attention to all this slows down the development of the action at the beginning of the film, just when it should be picking up momentum.) But what is relevant is that Mimi likes eggs with finely chopped liver, and that the grandmother has high blood pressure, which makes Serge insist that she stay in bed and promise that meals for her and her dog will be delivered the next day. This is the reason little Olivier sets out toward her house and becomes Marcel's victim. It is also necessary to show that the grandmother is a disagreeable person and her relationship with Elizabeth is not a good one—that's why Elizabeth does not find out immediately, and not from her, that Olivier never arrived at her house. And thus, the screenplay's entire first scene with the grandmother is condensed in the film into a few brief remarks between Serge and Elizabeth: "Mama isn't at all well, you know. . . . Tomorrow we'll have to bring Mama her meal. . . . Make her some eggs, with some finely chopped liver. . . . You know her whims."

The second scene with the grandmother was also omitted from the film: Nadine, some time after Olivier has vanished, visits the old lady, who is grieving Mimi's death and speaks of Olivier's disappearance as something of lesser importance. Here again we learn something about the grandmother, not about the story.

In the third scene, which is very brief, Serge is taking the grandmother to the nursing home. In the film, Serge simply tells Olivier about this, about her subsequent marriage to an old man, and about her recent death. Here this information is not given for her sake; she is used just as a topic to show how Serge enjoys a frank, "man-to-man" talk with his grown son.

Nadine, Olivier, and Elizabeth comprise a love triangle. Elizabeth obsessively loves Olivier: "My little lamb," she calls him, while she is almost indifferent, and sometimes even hostile to Nadine, whom she calls "My big girl." Nadine loves her mother and is jealous of Elizabeth's love for Olivier. Out of revenge, from time to time, she takes advantage of her younger brother and scares him with talk of monsters. But at the same time she cares for him. For his part, he generously allows both his mother and his sister to love him and take care of him.

With the second Olivier, the dynamics of this triangle change. Elizabeth adores him, as before, but his six-year absence has brought her closer to Nadine. "We were fine together, you were happy with me, you always said so," Nadine believes. But Elizabeth is really happy only now, when Olivier is back. Nadine is still jealous of her mother's love for Olivier, but now she is also suspicious of him. And, unlike little Olivier, he not only allows himself to be loved, but himself becomes fond of Elizabeth and falls in love with Nadine, which is why at the end he returns to them.

Serge Duval, the father, is outside of the triangle. Rather, he is a mirror in which the family's life, with all its disappointments, traumas, tragedies, and happy surprises, is reflected. A country vet, a modest, passive man without special talents or ambitions, Serge understands neither his sensitive, dreamy wife, nor Olivier—either as a little boy or as a teenager. And he certainly cannot understand his daughter, who is perceptive and intelligent beyond her years. "You never understand anything," Nadine says to him. In the film it's as if there are two Serges: one before Olivier's disappearance and his own departure for Africa—impatient, irritable, negative—that was the atmosphere of the family's daily life; and a different Serge when he returns, when both his outlook and his behavior have changed completely. Now he is a cheerful, agreeable man, a loving husband and attentive father.

At a certain point in the screenplay, Druot asks the young impostor why he pretended to be Olivier, to which the boy replies, "To make you [all] happy." This very happiness is reflected in Serge, a sense of uplifted spirits and parental joy at the "return" of their prodigal son.

The universe of *Olivier, Olivier* is rich with exquisite rural landscapes, forests, flowering fields of wheat and poppies, and a variety of animals: the monkey Serge gave to Nadine, the snake and hamster that live in her room, the chickens in the Duvals' backyard.

The animals in the film sometimes look and behave like people, and Serge is an animal doctor, to begin with. He gives an injection to his wife with the same syringe he used to give a shot to a cat. We learn in detail the particular tastes of the grandmother's dog, Mimi, who likes eggs with finely chopped liver.

Animals are also the precursors of events in the story: the crushed insect foreshadows Olivier's death; the cat with the syringe in its thigh, "charg[ing] through the room, yowling . . . making a terrible mess, knocking over vials and instruments," marks the start of the whirlwind of disorder, cries, emotions, and groans in the Duval household.

The animals also serve to create a certain kind of atmosphere. When Nadine, calling her brother in despair, sees cows in a pasture just outside the forest, they are described as "heavy, dark masses, they shake their heads and moo in the semidarkness." These images and sounds deepen the sense of heaviness and alarm. This scene was cut from the film, but another, similar scene was put in: Elizabeth, beside herself having just realized that Olivier has vanished, runs out into the fields, crying and calling her son. Her helplessness and despair are underscored by the indifferent, silent landscape, where cows are chewing monotonously beneath the huge, darkening sky. Her cries reverberate in the space. "My little lamb!" she cries. This tender expression of hers, which we have heard before, is now imbued with an additional meaning: Olivier, the sacrificial lamb, leads to a wider association of Mother grieving for her Son.

Agniezska Holland unfolds the action of *Olivier, Olivier* vigorously. Every scene moves the plot forward. She cannot stop and openly make a commentary on what is going on, as writers do to make a statement outside the story, to evaluate, poke fun, make a judgment or generalization, and then return to the action.

In film, voice-over can be used to bring in the author's commentary, but in *Olivier, Olivier* this device is not used. Holland makes her commentary nonverbally, through visual images. The screenplay suggests them. For example, when the little Olivier is riding his bicycle through the field of poppies, wearing his red cap, he himself seems to be one of the fragile, short-lived flowers. Or his empty swing, "swinging back and forth, against the darkness and rain." The last shot is beyond the story. Here Holland reminds us that the little boy is gone, his place is empty. But perhaps, if we take this swing image very broadly, we can say that every child's swing is painfully empty when that child grows up, changes, and the sweet little one vanishes forever.

Inga Karetnikova

I 1 – 19 – disappearance

II a) 19 – 31 – ~~aftermath~~ / life without O (family)

31 – 65 (??) Discovering Olivia

Disappearance

Return – life w/o O
Discovery O
(p. 46) = (seed of rejection)

Rejection

acceptance

Master Scene p. 38

(p. 49) = NOT OK

p. 46, 49 Discovery by Nadine